entrada

entrada

journeys in latin american cuisine

Bay Books is an imprint of Bay/SOMA Publishing, Inc.

444 De Haro St., Suite 130, San Francisco, CA 94107

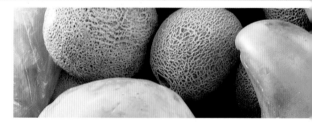

Publisher: James Connolly

Editorial Director: Floyd Yearout

Text: Joan Chatfield-Taylor

Managing Editor: Sarah Pirch

Indexer: Ken della Penta

Proofreader: Kendra Smith

Book Design: Terrace Partners

Selected Photographs: Roanna Sabeh-Azar

Library of Congress Cataloging-in-Publication
data available from the Publisher.
ISBN 1-57959-517-0

Printed in China

10 9 8 7 6 5 4 3 2 1

Distributed by Publishers Group West

Gourmet Excursions
The Way to Taste the World

CATALYST

GULLANE
ENTERTAINMENT

"Entrada: Journeys in Latin American Cuisine" is distributed by American Public Television in the United States.

Visit the world's most exotic locations in search of savory indigenous cuisine.

Come with *Entrada* on our Gourmet Excursion through Latin America, exploring the countryside and its food with host Roanna.

Inviting you on a Gourmet Excursion...

contents

Say the word Mexico, and tequila and mariachis come to mind. Add in the embroidered sombrero and the staccato rhythms of the Mexican hat dance, and you have a quartet of emblems known all over the world. All four were born in Guadalajara, the country's vibrant, sprawling second city. Five million people live here, guaranteeing that this is far more than a picturesque façade for tourists.

Guadalajara is a place to do as the Mexicans do, and that means taking advantage of a rich array of big-city cultural activities. Mariachis are everywhere, but they gather in large numbers on the Plaza de los Mariachis, where the bands come around and play for people sitting at outdoor cafes. Guadalajara residents also flock to performances of the Ballet Folklórico, which stamps and twirls in the red velvet confines of the Teatro Degollado. The Instituto Cultural de Cabañas offers a full schedule of concerts, theatrical performances, and dance festivals. It is also the setting for some of the finest murals executed by Guadalajara native son Jose Clemente Orozco.

The city's nightlife is rich and varied, making this a great place for salsa dancing and eating out. Eateries range from restaurants offering international cuisine to casual marisquerias that serve up platters of seafood and birrerias that offer the local specialty of slow-cooked goat in a spicy chile and tomato sauce. Whatever the fare, it's fine to wash it down with tequila. This most Mexican of spirits is made locally from the blue agave plant. In the nearby town of Tequila, it is possible to see the process of cutting out the center of the plant, steaming it for 24 hours, and then extracting the juice and letting it ferment, first in steel vats, then in oak barrels.

guadalajara

mexico

Guadalajara's cuisine benefits from its proximity to some of Mexico's most fertile land, watered by rivers and lakes. Its abundance is obvious at the Mercado Libertad, an immense indoor market where hundreds of stands overflow with tropical and temperate-climate fruits and vegetables, as well as beef from nearby ranches and fish from the Pacific and Lake Chapala.

chicken breast
with tequila, coconut, and pineapple

pechuga de pollo con tequila, coco y piña

This recipe presents some of Mexico's most exotic flavors—ginger, coconut, pineapple, and tequila—in a sauce that gives gently simmered chicken breasts the taste of the tropics.

2 chicken breasts

1 tablespoon vegetable oil

1/4 cup finely chopped white onion

1 teaspoon minced garlic

1/2 teaspoon minced fresh ginger

2 teaspoons ancho chile, fried, seeded, and sliced

1/3 cup grated fresh coconut

1/3 cup coarsely chopped fresh pineapple

2 ounces tequila

1/2 cup pineapple juice

1/4 cup tomato juice

Salt and pepper

2 teaspoons coarsely chopped cilantro

2 teaspoons grated Cotija cheese

In a 2- to 4-quart saucepan over medium-high heat, place chicken breasts in enough water to cover and bring to a boil. Reduce heat and simmer until just done, about 15 minutes. Remove from pan and keep warm.

In a 10- to 12-inch sauté pan over medium-high heat, warm oil. Add onion, garlic, and ginger and sauté until soft but not browned, about 7 minutes. Add chile strips, coconut, and chopped pineapple and simmer for 2 to 3 minutes, stirring constantly. Add the tequila and carefully flambé the mixture by immediately lighting the tequila fumes with a match and shaking pan until flames die down and alcohol is burned away. Stir in pineapple and tomato juices.

Add chicken breasts to pan and cook until heated, about 5 minutes. Season with salt and pepper to taste. Garnish with chopped cilantro and grated cheese and serve.

Serves 2

camarones flameados al tequila

shrimp flambéed
with tequila

Fresh shrimp, quickly cooked, are given the boost of one of Guadalajara's favorite flavors with the touch of a match to a generous splash of tequila. Pumpkin, garlic, onions, and cilantro round out the taste of this example of la nueva cocina mexicana.

1/3 cup olive oil

2 teaspoons chopped scallions, green parts only

4 teaspoons julienned pumpkin

1 teaspoon minced garlic

2 tablespoons chopped white onion

12 ounces peeled medium shrimp

1/2 teaspoon cayenne pepper

1 teaspoon paprika

3/4 cup tequila

4 teaspoons minced cilantro

1/4 cup lemon juice

Salt and pepper

2 cups cooked white rice

Warm olive oil over medium-high heat in a 10- to 12-inch sauté pan. Add scallions, pumpkin, garlic, and onion, and stir until onion is translucent and pumpkin is soft, about 5 minutes. Add shrimp and stir for 2 minutes. Add cayenne and paprika. Add tequila and heat to boiling point. Carefully light the tequila fumes with a match and shake pan until flames die down and alcohol is burned away. Add 2 teaspoons of the cilantro and all the lemon juice and season to taste with salt and pepper. Garnish with remaining cilantro and serve immediately with rice.

Serves 2

The mountainous ribbon that is Chile includes some of the most extreme geography on earth, from the towering glaciers and mountain meadows of the south to the Atacama Desert, one of the driest places on earth. In the semi-arid region called El Norte Chico, just south of the Atacama, the Elqui River flows from the snow-tipped Andes toward the beach resort of La Serena, turning its valley into an oasis of vineyards and orchards.

Grapes and figs aren't the only things that thrive here. With its astonishingly clear air, high levels of electromagnetic energy, and beauty and isolation, the Elqui Valley has become a New Age mecca. This is the place to try out holistic remedies, pyramid power, meditation, massage, and a host of other spiritual exercises.

For non-believers, the fertile valley offers other pleasures. Thanks to the dry, crystalline air, astronomers come here to visit several important observatories. Literary buffs make a pilgrimage to the town of Vicuña to visit the birthplace and museum of poet Gabriela Mistral, the first South American to win the Nobel Prize for Literature. Ecologists appreciate the world's first solar-powered restaurant, in the little town of Villa Seca, where food is prepared in foil-lined boxes fueled by nothing more than the sun. And connoisseurs of the grape head for the little town of Pisco Elqui, where vineyards filled with Muscat grapes produce a potent brandy that is often blended with egg whites, lime or lemon juice, and sugar to produce the deceptively innocent drink called a Pisco Sour.

elqui valley

chile

Chilean cooks have a choice of several different varieties of corn, some with ears a foot long. They use the kernels both cooked and uncooked, sometimes in the same dish for depth of flavor. They grind it up, for some quintessentially Chilean dishes like pastel de choclo and humitas, or cut it into chunks to put into cazuelas.

chilean chicken soup

cazuela de pollo

This hearty vegetable and potato soup is served as daily fare in Chilean restaurants and homes alike. Chilean cooks cut the chicken and vegetables into large pieces, because this soup is considered a meal in itself.

1 3- to 4-pound chicken, cut into 4 pieces

1 large carrot, peeled and cut into 1-inch pieces

1 large yellow onion, cut into 1-inch pieces

6 medium potatoes, peeled

1 pound squash, such as acorn or Hubbard, peeled and cut into 2-inch chunks

4 ears of corn, shucked and cut into 2-inch sections

1/2 red bell pepper, seeded and cut into thin strips

1 cup cornmeal

8 ounces green beans, cut into 2-inch sections

Salt and pepper

In a 12- to 16-quart pot over medium-high heat, place chicken pieces in enough water to cover and bring to a boil. Reduce heat and simmer for 20 minutes. Add carrot, onion, potatoes, squash, corn, and bell pepper and continue to simmer for 10 minutes. Add cornmeal slowly, stirring constantly. Add green beans. Add salt and pepper to taste, and cook for 10 more minutes. Serve immediately.

Serves 4

Humitas are the Chilean version of tamales. Both are tasty, savory or sweet packets of cornmeal wrapped in leaves—corn husks in temperate Chile, banana leaves in tropical climates—before being steamed or simmered.

12 ears corn
2 tablespoons lard or butter
1 white onion, finely chopped
2 large tomatoes, peeled, seeded, and chopped
Pinch sugar
Salt and pepper
2 tablespoons fresh basil, cut into strips
2 eggs
String

Husk corn, taking care not to break husks. Reserve husks to wrap humitas.

Cut kernels from corn and grind in a food processor or food mill; transfer to a large bowl.

In a 10- to 12-inch sauté pan, melt lard or butter. Add onion, tomatoes, sugar, and salt and pepper to taste. Cook over medium heat for 10 minutes, stirring occasionally. Add this mixture to corn. Add basil and eggs, stirring to combine well.

Lay corn husks flat. In the center of each husk, place 3 tablespoons of corn mixture. Fold corn husks over into rectangular packages approximately 3 inches by 2 inches. Tie with string (as shown above left). Simmer packages in salted water for 40 minutes.

Serves 6

seasoned ground corn
steamed in corn husks

humitas

chilean baked empanadas

empanadas de horno

The empanada, a crescent of pastry filled with a mixture of meat or cheese, is a classic dish throughout much of South America. Although empanadas are most delicious when served hot, they're also a popular picnic food to be eaten on the sidelines of a polo match in Argentina or at a rodeo in Chile. To be totally authentic, empanadas should have a decorative edging resembling rope.

filling:

3 tablespoons olive oil

8 ounces beef sirloin or 1 large chicken breast, cut into 1/2-inch cubes

1 large onion, finely chopped

1 teaspoon red pepper flakes

1/2 teaspoon cumin

2 tablespoons flour

2 tablespoons raisins

Salt and pepper

pastry:

2 cups flour

1/2 cup butter, melted

2 egg yolks, lightly beaten

1 1/2 teaspoons salt

2 hardboiled eggs, each cut into 6 sections lengthwise

12 pitted olives, halved

1 egg and 1/4 cup water, mixed together

Preheat oven to 400°F. To make the filling, warm olive oil over medium-high heat in a 10- to 12-inch sauté pan. Add diced sirloin or chicken and brown, stirring frequently. Remove from pan with a slotted spoon and reserve. In the same pan, over medium-high heat, sauté onion, red pepper flakes, and cumin until onion is translucent, about 5 minutes, stirring occasionally. Return meat to pan and stir in flour. Add raisins, 1 cup hot water, and salt and pepper to taste. Simmer for 10 minutes.

To prepare the pastry, sift flour into a large bowl. Make a well in the middle and place melted butter and egg yolks into the well. Add 1/2 cup hot water and salt, and mix thoroughly. Form dough into a ball and roll out on a lightly floured surface to a thickness of about 1/4 inch. Cut into circles 5 inches in diameter, using a cookie cutter or an empty can.

On each circle of dough, place 2 heaping tablespoons of filling, a section of hardboiled egg, and 2 olive halves, leaving 1/2 inch of dough exposed at the edges. Moisten the edges with water and fold the filled pastry in half. Shape the folded pastry into a crescent, pressing the edges together into a decorative edging.

Place empanadas on lightly buttered and floured baking sheet. With a pastry brush, brush each pastry with egg and water mixture. Bake for 25 to 30 minutes, until pastry is golden brown. Serve at once.

makes 12 to 14

The road to Monteverde is steep, narrow, and punctuated by rocks that break axles and burst tires. Nevertheless, no one is pushing hard to smooth it out, because the two-hour climb from the Pan-American Highway protects a unique community and a distinctive ecosystem from casual visitors. Perched at an altitude of 5,600 feet, Monteverde is a cloud forest, a cool-weather jungle wrapped in mist and buffeted by wind. Several wildlife preserves protect one of the most species-diverse areas in the world, home to 100 species of mammals, 2,600 different kinds of birds, countless insects, and some 2,500 plant species, including 420 types of orchids.

Walking along the cloud forest's slippery trails is a fantastic experience, so rich in detail that it hardly matters if one never sees the real rarities, like the jaguar or the long-tailed Resplendent Quetzal. The vegetation—towering ferns and bromeliads, swinging vines, tree-swallowing strangler figs—is so thick that sunlight barely reaches the forest floor. Howler monkeys screech high in the canopy, and flights of brilliantly colored hummingbirds and butterflies flicker in the dim light. Orchids, growing in the bark of trees, bloom spectacularly but sometimes for only a day or two. Everything seems to be growing and dying and rotting at an unsettling speed.

Monteverde is also a unique human community—a blend of Costa Ricans and the descendants of a group of American Quakers who moved here in the 1950s. Together they have worked to protect Monteverde's rich environmental heritage through ecologically sustainable tourism. Local landowners have found that a nature trail through a landscape rich in birds and butterflies can be more profitable than cattle raising or farming.

monteverde

costa rica

The Quakers who settled near the Monteverde Cloud Forest have influenced the way people eat and raise food in the area. After the Quakers had established their cattle-raising operations, they created a cheese-making factory that sells cheese and ice cream locally and around the country. Numerous organic farms, including a coffee plantation, have also been established in the area to provide fruits and vegetables to local restaurants and residents.

stuffed seabass
in a mussel cream sauce

corvina rellena con crema de mejillones

The coast is never far away in Costa Rica, so chef Hugo Salas of the Monteverde Lodge has combined fresh seabass with a smoked cheese manufactured by the Quakers' cheese factory and eggplant from one of the many local farms.

1 7-ounce seabass fillet

2 tablespoons lemon juice

2 cloves garlic, minced

Salt and pepper

1 tablespoon cornstarch

1 cup fish stock

1/2 cup olive oil, plus 1 tablespoon

1 cup peeled and diced eggplant

1 tablespoon fresh basil, cut into strips

1/2 cup grated smoked mozzarella cheese

1/4 cup grated parmesan cheese

1 teaspoon paprika

1 celery stalk, finely chopped

8 mussels in shells, cleaned and debearded

1/4 cup white wine

1/4 cup cream

Marinate fish fillet in lemon juice, half the garlic, and salt and pepper to taste for 5 minutes.

Stir cornstarch into 1/4 cup of the fish stock and set aside.

In a 10- to 12-inch sauté pan over medium-high heat, warm 1/4 cup of the olive oil and sauté eggplant and basil, stirring frequently, until eggplant is very soft, about 10 minutes.

Slice fish fillet almost in half horizontally and fill cavity with eggplant mixture and grated mozzarella cheese. Mix parmesan cheese with paprika in a shallow dish. Roll fish fillet in mixture to coat. In same sauté pan over medium-high heat, sauté fish fillet in 1 tablespoon of the olive oil, approximately 5 minutes on each side.

Warm remaining 1/4 cup olive oil in a 4- to 6-quart pan over medium heat. Add celery, the remaining garlic, and mussels and cook for 1 minute. Add wine and let boil for 1 minute. Add remaining fish stock and cream; reduce heat to medium and cook for 4 minutes. Stir the fish stock and cornstarch mixture and add to pan to thicken sauce. Spoon sauce over fish fillet and serve immediately.

Serves 1

Argentina has become the fifth largest wine producer in the world. In recent years, winemakers from California, Spain, and France have established their own vineyards here. Since their arrival, the quality of the wine produced has increased dramatically, so that the country's refined wines are now suitable for export.

In addition to familiar European varietals like Cabernet Sauvignon and Pinot Noir, Argentine vintners grow the Malbec grape. Considered a minor blending element in Bordeaux, it takes on a different, richer, and more velvety quality in the temperate climate and sandy soil of Argentina's Mendoza province. Malbec is now considered the finest wine in the country.

The place to taste it is the city of Mendoza, 470 miles west of Buenos Aires, where the snow-frosted peaks of the Andes rise abruptly from the plains. In the last few years, this pretty city of 600,000 people, almost half of Italian descent, has taken on an international gloss.

In addition to being a showplace for wine, Mendoza is a sports center— the jumping-off place for hikers, mountain climbers, skiers, horseback riders, and river rafters lured by the challenging terrain and rushing rivers of the Andes. Mount Aconcagua, at 6,959 meters the tallest mountain in the Western hemisphere, is directly west of the city. More leisurely activities include bathing in the area's thermal pools, strolling along the 17 kilometers of trails in the city's tranquil San Martín Park, and sampling wine in congenial cafes.

mendoza

argentina

The unchallenged star of the Argentine diet is grass-fed beef from the Pampas, which some people eat several times a day. But a vegetarian could be happy in the city of Mendoza. Farmers have irrigated the once-arid plains of the Cuyo region, taking advantage of runoff from the mountains to grow a wide variety of fruits, vegetables, nuts, and grains.

beef and veal stew

in a pumpkin

carbonada en zapallo

One of Argentina's most traditional dishes strikes a balance between meat and chunks of vegetables and peaches, all cooked up in an enormous pumpkin and flavored with a savory sauce of pancetta, onions, fresh herbs, and red pepper. If a pumpkin won't fit in your oven, a heavy casserole will suffice.

meat and broth:

2 pounds veal shank

2 pounds beef brisket

6 cups vegetable stock

1 clove garlic, peeled

pumpkin:

1 whole pumpkin, at least 12 inches wide

4 tablespoons unsalted butter

1 tablespoon sugar

1/2 cup milk

Salt and pepper

stew:

4 large boiling potatoes, peeled and cut into 2-inch pieces

4 sweet potatoes, peeled and cut into 2-inch pieces

4 peaches, peeled, pitted, and quartered

6 large tomatoes, peeled, seeded, and quartered

1 pound pumpkin or acorn squash, peeled and cut into 2-inch pieces

3 ears corn, cut into 2-inch sections

2 sprigs thyme

1 sprig rosemary

2 sprigs parsley

1 bay leaf

1 teaspoon red pepper flakes

Salt and pepper

2 tablespoons olive oil

2 large onions, sliced

sauce:

4 ounces pancetta or bacon, cooked until crisp and finely chopped

2 green onions, finely chopped

1 red bell pepper, seeded, deribbed, and finely chopped

1 sprig each thyme, rosemary, and parsley, minced

1 tablespoon paprika

1/2 cup olive oil

In a 10- to 12-quart pot over high heat, place veal, beef, vegetable stock, and garlic. Bring to a boil, then reduce heat to low and cook, covered, for 3 hours. Transfer meat to a bowl and let cool slightly. Remove meat from bones, remove gristle and fat, and shred meat. Strain the cooking liquid into a bowl; set aside.

Preheat oven to 350°F. Cut a large circle in the top of the whole pumpkin; remove the top. Clean the seeds and fibers from the pumpkin and score the interior flesh lightly with a knife. Put butter, sugar, and milk inside. Season with salt and pepper to taste. Replace the top. Bake pumpkin until the skin is hard and the flesh tender, about 45 minutes.

To make the stew, place boiling potatoes, sweet potatoes, peaches, tomatoes, pumpkin, corn, thyme, rosemary, parsley, bay leaf, red pepper flakes, and salt and pepper to taste in the pot you cooked the meat in. Add water to cover and cook, covered with a lid, over medium heat until vegetables are tender, about 30 minutes. Drain stew and set aside, discarding liquid.

In a 10- to 12-inch sauté pan, warm olive oil over medium-high heat. Add sliced onions, reduce heat to medium and cook until onions are soft, stirring occasionally.

To make the sauce, combine pancetta or bacon, green onions, bell pepper, thyme, rosemary, parsley, paprika, and olive oil in a small saucepan. Cook over medium heat for 5 minutes, stirring often.

To assemble the carbonada, layer the meat and the stew inside the cooked pumpkin shell and pour 2 cups of the reserved cooking liquid over the filling. Spread the sauce over the filling, place top on pumpkin, and return to oven for 20 minutes. Serve carbonada directly from pumpkin, making sure that each person gets a little of each meat and vegetable.

Serves 6

The very idea of Mexico City is intimidating. The city has grown so fast that it is hard to get a precise population figure, but it's estimated that some 22 million people are crowded into this 7,400-foot-high valley, with more arriving everyday. Like any big city, Mexico City has experienced crowding, poverty, air pollution, and crime. Nevertheless, the city is a thrilling, fascinating place, where moments of tranquillity and pleasure abound.

One dependable refuge is the famous Anthropology Museum, a magnificent modern building opened in 1964. Here, Mexico's earliest history comes to life through some of the nation's most powerful symbols, including the Aztec calendar stone and the Toltec Chac-Mool sculpture, displayed in rooms devoted to different areas of the country.

Another place of relative calm is the ornate Palacio de Bellas Artes, where controversial Diego Rivera murals, the Ballet Folklórico, and the National Symphony vie for attention.

A few quiet, upscale neighborhoods—small towns within the big city—offer the chance to walk on cobblestone streets, shop at stylish small boutiques, and drink a cappuccino at a sidewalk cafe. San Angel is the setting for an outdoor crafts market every Sunday, and Coyoacán invites visitors to see the homes of two former residents, artist Frida Kahlo and Russian revolutionary Leon Trotsky.

Some fortunate residents of the megalopolis escape even farther on weekends, driving 80 miles southwest to the little town of Malinalco, ringed by mountains and fruit orchards. Boasting both an intact Aztec ruin and charming colonial houses, the town is stirring with new shops and artists' studios.

mexico city

mexico

Mexico City has been a center for elaborate cooking since the Aztecs enhanced the basic ingredients—corn, beans, and chiles—with chocolate, cactus, avocados, turkey, and sweet potatoes. The Aztec diet survives throughout the country, but the capital's sophisticated restaurants show the extent to which it has been enriched by the Spanish conquistadores' contributions and refined by contact with French and other world cuisines.

For a dessert as spectacular as a sunset, chill this suave mixture of fruit and sour cream in a ring mold, turn it out on a bright yellow serving plate, and surround it with fresh berries dusted with a sprinkling of powdered sugar.

4 tablespoons unflavored gelatin
1/2 cup fresh orange juice
1 tablespoon lemon juice
2 cups mango pulp
3/4 cup sour cream
1/4 cup plain yogurt
About 2/3 cup sugar
2 tablespoons dark rum
Fresh berries

Place gelatin in a small, heavy-bottomed saucepan and add orange and lemon juices. Over low heat, stir mixture until gelatin is dissolved. Reserve.

In a blender or food processor, purée mango pulp, sour cream, yogurt, sugar, and rum. Add gelatin mixture and mix briefly. Depending on the sweetness of the fruit, you may want to add more sugar at this time.

Put mango-gelatin mixture into a 6-cup ring mold. Refrigerate until set, 3 to 4 hours. To unmold mousse, loosen around the edges with a knife, place serving plate on top of mold, and flip over. If mousse does not drop down onto plate, place a hot, wet dishtowel on the mold to warm it so the mousse slides out. Serve cold, with fresh berries.

Serves 6 to 8

mango mousse

mousse de mango

smoked salmon carpaccio
with tequila and salsa verde

The capital's urbane restaurants offer food that combines European and Mexican ingredients and techniques. The classic luxury of smoked salmon is given a thoroughly local flavor with the addition of a few splashes of tequila and a green chile salsa on the side.

carpaccio de salmón ahumado con tequila y salsa verde

1¼ pounds smoked salmon

⅓ to ½ cup tequila

1 cup tomatillos, husked and chopped

2 to 3 serrano chiles, seeded

¼ cup chopped white onion

2 tablespoons cilantro

½ small clove garlic

1 tablespoon olive oil

Salt

Cilantro sprigs for garnish

⅓ cup finely chopped green onions or shallots

Tortilla chips or toasted pita bread

Slightly overlap slices of smoked salmon on a platter and drizzle with tequila. Cover with plastic wrap and refrigerate for at least 10 minutes or until ready to use.

Using a mortar and pestle or a food processor, blend tomatillos, chiles, onion, cilantro, garlic, olive oil, and salt to taste.

Place salmon on serving plate, top with dollops of tomatillo mixture. Sprinkle with cilantro sprigs and chopped green onions or shallots. Serve with tortilla chips or toasted pita bread and remaining tomatillo mixture on the side.

Serves 6

poblano chiles
stuffed with shrimp and corn salad

chiles poblanos rellenos de camarones y ensalada de maíz

Mexico City's most interesting restaurants offer the visitor the chance to try sophisticated versions of classic Mexican recipes, like this one for shrimp-filled chiles, here given a rich and subtle sauce flavored with anchovies and garlic.

dressing:

1 head garlic

1¼ cups plus about 2 tablespoons olive oil

2 egg yolks

¼ teaspoon Dijon mustard

½ teaspoon lemon juice

1 tablespoon red wine vinegar

3 anchovy fillets, mashed

½ teaspoon Worcestershire sauce

¼ teaspoon minced garlic

1 tablespoon finely grated Cotija or parmesan cheese

2 tablespoons Crema Mexicana or heavy cream

Salt and pepper

6 fresh poblano chiles

salad:

½ cup fresh lime juice

3 teaspoons ground coriander

5 tablespoons extra-virgin olive oil

30 large shrimp, peeled and deveined

Salt and pepper

3 ears fresh corn, preferably white, husk and silk removed

2 small jalapeño chiles, seeded, deribbed, and minced

3 medium shallots, minced

3 to 4 tablespoons minced cilantro

Mesquite wood chips (soaked in water)

garnish:

1 medium avocado, cut in ½-inch cubes

Minced cilantro

To prepare dressing, preheat oven to 250°F. Slice ¼ inch off the top of the head of garlic. Drizzle the head with about 2 tablespoons of the olive oil and wrap tightly in foil. Bake in the oven until soft, 40 to 50 minutes; let cool. Squeeze each clove into a small bowl to remove the roasted pulp from the papery outer layer; set aside.

In a medium bowl, stir together egg yolks and mustard. Slowly add 1¼ cups of the olive oil in a very thin stream, whisking constantly until a thick, emulsified sauce forms. Stir in lemon juice and vinegar, followed by anchovies, Worcestershire sauce, minced garlic, Cotija or parmesan cheese, Crema Mexican or cream, salt and pepper to taste, and the roasted garlic. The dressing can be prepared a day ahead and refrigerated.

Wash and dry chiles. Place chiles directly over a medium gas flame and turn them frequently until they are blackened. Be careful not to overcook as they will tear. Place chiles in a paper or plastic bag, close the bag, and let them sweat for 15 to 20 minutes. Remove chiles from bag and carefully peel off skin, rubbing under cold running water.

To make the salad, in a medium bowl, combine 6 tablespoons of the lime juice, 1½ teaspoons of the ground coriander, 3 tablespoons of the olive oil, all the shrimp, and salt and pepper to taste. Cover the bowl with plastic wrap and place in the refrigerator for 30 minutes.

Heat barbecue to medium-high and add mesquite chips. Brush grill with olive oil. Brush corn with remaining olive oil, sprinkle with salt and pepper, and grill, turning until golden, 12 to 18 minutes; let cool. Remove shrimp from marinade and grill until they are opaque and cooked through, 2 to 4 minutes. Cut shrimp into ¼-inch pieces and place in a bowl. When corn is cool, slice kernels off ears and add to bowl. Add jalapeño, shallots, cilantro, and remaining 2 tablespoons lime juice, 1½ teaspoons ground coriander, and 2 tablespoons olive oil, and salt and pepper to taste. Mix gently, cover with plastic wrap, and refrigerate.

To assemble the chiles, carefully make a slit down the side of each chile. Fill each chile with shrimp and corn salad. Drizzle with dressing and garnish with avocado and cilantro. Serve at room temperature.

Serves 6

In Chile, the cowboy is called a huaso, and he has his own distinctive costume, culture, and even cuisine.

Like the Argentine guachos, he rides a sturdy horse called a criollo, descendant of the herd of Spanish steeds imported to Argentina some four centuries ago. These horses, short and broad chested, are known for their endurance in extreme climates and their ability to survive with a minimum of food. In Chile's Central Valley, huasos and their criollos show off their skills at rodeos where the emphasis is on the coordination between rider and horse rather than roping or riding broncos. A pair of cowboys work together, their horses moving forward and sideways with astonishing speed and agility, to force a steer up against a padded fence. This Chilean version of the American cowboy's cutting horse contest is a stylized refinement of working cattle on the range.

Afterwards, the huaso, whose traditional costume includes knee-high boots, a flat-brimmed, flat-crowned hat, and a short, striped poncho, shows off his social skills, performing the cueca—the flirtatious footwork that's the official national dance of Chile. These traditions date from the days of the great colonial estancias, or ranches. And despite the modernization of Chile's countryside, traditions like these remain popular in the Central Valley.

central valley

chile

Chile, narrow and mountainous, has extreme climates both north and south.
These geographical differences provide a balanced diet, featuring fish, meat, and the
vegetables and fruit that grow in such abundance in the middle third of the country.

vegetable and beef
jerky stew

charquicán

Charquicán is a traditional Chilean dish, combining a relatively small amount of meat—ideally, beef jerky that's been rehydrated in water—and a rainbow of vegetables, from pumpkin and peppers to peas and corn, bathed in a sauce that's flavorful, not hot.

1 pound beef jerky or ground beef

8 large boiling potatoes, peeled

1 pound mixed vegetables, including carrots, peas, pumpkin, and red bell pepper

2 cups fresh corn kernels

2 cups beef or chicken stock

Salt

3 tablespoons lard or vegetable oil

1 onion, sliced

1 teaspoon paprika

Pinch of cayenne

1 teaspoon oregano

1/2 teaspoon cumin

Pepper

Hot salsa

To rehydrate beef jerky, soak it in water overnight. The next day, cut it into very small pieces. Or, brown ground beef and proceed immediately with recipe.

Cut larger vegetables into 1-inch pieces. In a 12- to 16-quart pot over high heat, place chicken stock and all vegetables and bring to a boil. Season to taste with salt. Reduce heat and simmer for 15 minutes.

Meanwhile, warm lard or vegetable oil in a heavy 12- to 14-inch sauté pan over medium-high heat. Add meat and onion and sauté for 5 minutes. Add paprika, cayenne, oregano, cumin, and pepper. Cook for 3 more minutes, stirring occasionally. Add the beef mixture to the vegetables and cook on low heat, uncovered, stirring occasionally, until the liquid evaporates, 15 to 20 minutes.

This is traditionally served with hot salsa on the side.

Serves 6

black olive soup

sopa de aceitunas negras

Cooks in Chile like to use black azapa olives from the northern part of their country, but North American cooks should experiment with various kinds of Mediterranean olives, using one type or several for complex flavor.

2 pounds black olives

1 quart homemade chicken stock

1 teaspoon dried oregano

1 teaspoon cumin

4 tablespoons heavy cream

Salt and pepper

Pit olives and chop the pulp very fine by hand or using a food processor. Place chicken stock in a 2- to 3-quart saucepan and add olives, oregano, cumin, cream, and salt and pepper to taste.

Bring to a boil over medium heat. Can be served hot or chilled.

Serves 4 to 6

Costa Rican geography is a simple matter of mountains—actually four mountain ranges squeezed between two oceans. The area around the capital city of San José, known as the Central Valley, is a tumultuous patchwork of gorges, terraced hillsides, and gently puffing volcanoes, all dressed in intense shades of green. This is where two-thirds of Costa Rica's population lives, attracted by the healthy climate and mineral-rich volcanic soil.

Even on the steepest slopes, the shiny leaves of coffee bushes shimmer in the sunlight. High-grade coffee, which needs a precise formula of sun, rain, earth, altitude, and shade, has been the principal crop here since the mid-nineteenth century, attracting foreign settlers and creating a larger middle class than exists in other Central American countries.

Coffee prices, however, are variable, and Costa Rican entrepreneurs have had to come up with other ways to make money in this lovely landscape. Butterfly farming, for instance, may sound frivolous, but it has turned into a multimillion-dollar business of exporting pupae to butterfly exhibits around the world.

High-wheeled oxcarts, brilliantly painted with fruit and flower designs, as small as a lemon or as large as an SUV, are the specialty of the crafts town of Sarchí. Cumbersome as they may look, they, too, are an export item because they can be knocked down flat to be reassembled in gardens and rec rooms.

White-water rafting on the Reventazón River and exploring for the neon blue Morpho butterfly at Braulio Carrillo National Park are other ways for visitors to appreciate the natural beauty of this lofty tropical paradise.

central valley

costa rica

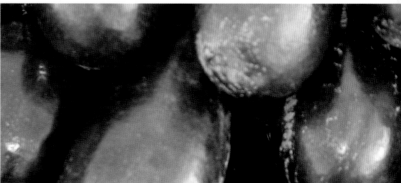

Although coffee is the most important cash crop on the high plateau of Costa Rica, the many outdoor produce stands that line the Pan-American Highway are proof that these rippling hillsides are capable of producing a wide variety of fruits and vegetables. Squash, corn, hearts of palm, plantains, pineapples, watermelon, berries, mangos, and papayas brighten up the Costa Rican basics—rice, beans, and tortillas.

estofado de res

coffee goulash

The population of Costa Rica is mostly of Spanish descent, and the favorite foods are only mildly spiced in comparison with their neighbor to the north, Mexico. This delicate beef stew shows its European background in its use of butter and wine, but a jolt of espresso coffee gives it a special Costa Rican flavor.

4 tablespoons butter

1 pound beef tenderloin, cut into 1/2-inch cubes

1 clove garlic, minced

1 medium carrot, coarsely chopped

2 small onions, coarsely chopped

1 1/2 tablespoons flour

2 pinches marjoram

1/4 cup freshly brewed espresso coffee

1 cup red wine

Salt and pepper

Hot cooked pasta

In a 2- to 4-quart heavy saucepan over high heat, melt the butter. Sauté the meat on all sides. Add the garlic, carrot, and onions and sauté until golden. Remove meat, garlic, carrot, and onions and keep them warm, reserving butter in pan. Reduce heat to low; add flour to the pan and stir it into the butter. Increase heat to medium and add 1/2 cup water, marjoram, and coffee. Stir until the sauce thickens slightly. Add wine and meat mixture to pan; season with salt and pepper to taste. Cover and simmer gently for 1 hour. Serve with pasta.

Serves 4

coffee mousse

mousse de café

This mousse recipe has a double whammy of coffee flavor—the espresso folded into the eggs and sugar, plus chocolate-covered coffee beans as a sweet and caffeinated garnish.

4 eggs

2 tablespoons gelatin

1/2 cup freshly brewed espresso coffee

1/3 cup superfine sugar

1 cup whipping cream

Whipped cream for garnish

Chocolate-covered coffee beans

Separate the eggs. In a medium bowl, beat the whites until they form soft peaks.

In another medium bowl, dilute the gelatin in 1/4 cup water; add espresso, sugar, and egg yolks and beat until smooth. In another medium bowl, whip cream until it forms soft peaks; fold into coffee mixture. Then fold in beaten egg whites.

Spoon into 4 individual dessert cups or glasses and refrigerate for 2 hours. Just before serving, decorate with a spoonful of whipped cream and a few chocolate-covered coffee beans.

Serves 4

tortilla and egg sandwiches
with creole sauce

Nothing complicated here, just the crispness of a freshly fried tortilla, a gently cooked egg, and a fresh tomato sauce—just the thing for a leisurely weekend breakfast, with great Costa Rican coffee and tropical fruit juice as the perfect accompaniments.

huevos a caballo con salsa criolla

1/4 cup plus 2 tablespoons olive oil

1 white onion, chopped

1 red bell pepper, seeded, deribbed, and chopped

1 large tomato, peeled, seeded and chopped

2 tablespoons minced cilantro

Salt and pepper

4 corn tortillas

2 eggs

In a 10- to 12-inch sauté pan, warm 2 tablespoons of the olive oil over medium-high heat. Add onion and bell pepper and cook until onion is translucent. Add tomato, cilantro, and salt and pepper to taste. Cook over medium heat for 10 minutes.

In a large sauté pan, warm remaining 1/4 cup of the olive oil over medium-high heat. Place two tortillas in oil and brown lightly. Crack an egg on each tortilla. When the eggs are partially cooked, top each with another tortilla. Flip over each sandwich and cook until second tortilla is crisp and egg is cooked. Top each sandwich with tomato sauce.

Serves 2

When Spanish explorer Pedro de Mendoza first set foot on the shore of the Rio de la Plata in 1536, he was the first of millions of immigrants who created Latin America's most European city, Buenos Aires. Although the Spanish dominated the first three centuries of the city's history, they were eventually followed by waves of Italians, English, Jews, and Middle Easterners. They settled in a city filled with visual reminders of Paris.

Like Baron Haussmann in the French capital, Buenos Aires' mayors slashed through narrow, convoluted streets and modest one-story neighborhoods to create wide boulevards lined with iron-balconied apartment buildings. The city's most obvious symbol, the obelisk that stands in the center of Plaza de la Republica to commemorate Mendoza's arrival, is a reminder of the obelisk on the Place Vendome. And the Galerias Pacifico echoes another glass-roofed shopping arcade, Paris' Galerie Vivienne. The Teatro Colón, an opera house as luxurious as any in Europe, has been welcoming the greatest opera singers in the world since 1908, when the theater opened with a performance of Verdi's *Aida*.

The city's fondness for its European ancestry is reflected in more intimate ways. The outdoor cafe, with its breakfasts of café au lait and croissants, is an essential part of life in a cosmopolitan city. The high quality of the ice cream in the city's many heladerias is attributed to the descendants of Italian immigrants. With its soft "zh" sounds, even the distinctive form of Spanish spoken by the porteños, as the residents of Buenos Aires are called, has been influenced by the pronunciation of waves of Italian immigrants.

buenos aires

argentina

Buenos Aires residents love their parrillas, restaurants specializing in grilled meats. But this sophisticated city of immigrants also offers pizza and pasta, Cantonese sweet and sour pork, and boeuf bourguignon, as well as occasional forays into la nueva cocina latina, which blends European techniques and local products. Whatever the cuisine, dining hours are Spanish, with porteños sitting down for dinner as late as midnight and finishing up their last bite of flan in the wee hours of the morning.

braised quail
with white wine and green peppercorns

codorniz con vino blanco y pimienta verde

Hunters come from all over the world to shoot quail and dove on the broad expanses of Argentina's pampas. This recipe, which cooks browned quail gently in a vegetable-perfumed broth, might be served at the end of a long day of hunting at an estancia, the name for the large cattle ranches that spread across the pampas.

2 tablespoons butter

4 quails, cleaned

1 cup white wine

2 tablespoons green peppercorns

1 teaspoon coarse salt

1 sprig thyme

1 sprig sage

1 bay leaf

1 medium white onion, coarsely chopped

1 leek, white part only, sliced

3 medium carrots, sliced

5 cups vegetable stock

Preheat oven to 400°F.

In a heavy 8- to 10-quart casserole with a lid over medium-high heat, melt butter and brown quails. Add white wine and let bubble for 2 to 3 minutes. Add green peppercorns, salt, thyme, sage, bay leaf, onion, leek, and carrots. Cover with vegetable stock. Cover the ingredients with a piece of wax paper with a 2-inch circle cut in the middle. Cover casserole with its lid and bake in the oven for 50 minutes. When the quails are tender, remove from liquid, discarding vegetables, and serve.

Serves 4

stuffed portobello mushrooms

hongos rellenos

This recipe pays tribute to Buenos Aires' Italian heritage, combining meaty portobello mushrooms with a rich stuffing flavored with basil, parsley, almonds, pistachios, and provolone cheese. Although chef Pablo Massey serves it as an appetizer, it's substantial enough for a light lunch.

8 large portobello mushrooms

1/2 cup minced parsley

1/4 cup minced basil

2 cups bread crumbs

1/2 cup grated provolone cheese

1/2 cup coarsely chopped pistachios

1/2 cup coarsely chopped almonds

Salt and freshly ground pepper

4 tablespoons cold butter, chopped

4 tablespoons olive oil

1/4 cup soy sauce or teriyaki sauce

Preheat oven to 400°F.

Separate the stems from the mushroom caps and chop the stems coarsely. In a medium bowl, combine chopped mushroom stems, parsley, basil, bread crumbs, cheese, pistachios, almonds, and salt and freshly ground pepper to taste. Add cold butter. Chill in the refrigerator while preparing mushroom caps.

In a large sauté pan over medium-high heat, warm the olive oil and sauté the mushroom caps until barely tender; turn once, cooking for about 3 minutes on each side, adding soy or teriyaki sauce just before removing from heat. Arrange the mushroom caps in a baking pan, gill-side up, fill them with the nut mixture, and bake for 20 minutes or until the top of the nut mixture is golden.

Serves 8

Spanish priests are credited with planting the first wine grapes in Chile sometime around 1535. For the next 300 years, there was plenty of sacramental wine and vin ordinaire, most of it made from a very ordinary grape called País. In the mid-1850s, Silvestre Ochagavia, father of the modern wine industry in Chile, recognized that its volcanic soil and temperate climate, similar to that of Bordeaux, were capable of greater things. He imported both French vines and French winemakers to raise the standards of Chilean vineyards. Their efforts were a success. Chilean wines, particularly Cabernet Sauvignon, gained respect and a place in the world market.

Today, there's a further move toward higher quality and greater diversification in the Central Valley, where the country's best vineyards nestle between the coastal mountains and the Andes. Top French winemakers, along with Spanish and Californian rivals, have bought their own vineyards or entered into joint ventures in Chile. They brought with them friendly competition, high standards, and the latest winemaking technology. They also have sparked an increase in the range of grape varieties, trying out Pinot Noir, Cabernet Franc, Sangiovese, Syrah, and Viognier grapes.

In spite of modernization, the Central Valley remains a place to get a glimpse of the times of the colonial aristocracy, when the rich lived in spacious haciendas filled with European antiques and paintings. Their expansive ranchos, a day or more by horse-drawn carriage from the capital of Santiago, were self-sufficient kingdoms, with hundreds of workers producing everything from meat to bricks. Visitors came for weeks, sitting down every night at long tables set with heavy silver and fine porcelain.

wine country chile

The face of the Chilean wine industry is changing. The joint ventures with foreign winemakers—such as Eric and Philippe de Rothschild from Bordeaux and Robert Mondavi from California—have raised the level of both grape-growing and winemaking. Now, some of the best Chilean growers are opting to make their own estate-bottled vintages rather than selling their grapes to giant wineries.

seafood pie
with corn topping

pastel de choclo a la chilota

Think of this as the Chilean version of shepherd's pie, with a thick crust of lightly browned, puréed corn instead of mashed potatoes. Although it is most often made with meat, this version combines a medley of seafood with a bit of spicy chorizo sausage.

filling:

1 cup dry white wine

3 pounds mussels, cleaned and debearded

3 pounds clams

3 tablespoons butter or vegetable oil

5-inch link of chorizo, coarsely chopped

3/4 cup finely chopped onion

3 scallions, finely chopped

1 teaspoon sweet paprika

Pinch of cayenne pepper

2 tablespoons all-purpose flour

1 tablespoon minced parsley

Salt and pepper

corn topping:

11 cups corn kernels, fresh or frozen

3/4 cup milk

12 large basil leaves

4 tablespoons butter

Salt and freshly ground pepper

1 large egg, lightly beaten

12 medium shrimp, peeled

12 to 16 bay scallops or 6 sea scallops, halved

12 green olives

Hot salsa

Preheat oven to 375°F. In a 10- to 12-quart pot, bring white wine and 1 cup water to a boil over high heat. Add mussels and cover. Cook for 3 to 5 minutes, stirring once or twice, until mussels are wide open. Remove mussels with a slotted spoon to a colander set on a large plate. Add clams to the cooking liquid, and cook in the same manner until they open. Remove with a slotted spoon to colander. Add any liquid that has collected in the plate to the cooking liquid and reserve. When mussels and clams are cool enough to handle, remove meat from shells and set aside. Discard any that do not open.

Melt butter or warm vegetable oil in a 4- to 6-quart saucepan over medium heat. Add chorizo, onion, and scallions, and sauté for 3 to 4 minutes, stirring occasionally. Season with paprika and cayenne. Sprinkle flour on the mixture, and gradually stir in 11/2 cups of the cooking liquid. Bring to a boil and cook, stirring, until thickened, about 2 minutes. Add the parsley, taste for seasonings, and add salt and pepper if necessary.

To make the corn topping, in a blender or food processor, purée corn in batches with the milk and basil. For a smooth, pastry-like consistency, press it through a sieve. Melt butter in a 12- to 14-inch sauté pan over medium heat. Add corn purée and season with salt and pepper. While stirring constantly, add the egg. Continue to stir over low heat until the mixture thickens slightly, 3 to 4 minutes.

Divide the mussels, clams, shrimp, and scallops among six 2-cup earthenware dishes. Ladle chorizo sauce over each serving, and place 2 olives in each dish. Cover the ingredients with the corn topping. Bake until topping is lightly browned, about 10 minutes.

This is traditionally served with a hot salsa on the side.

Serves 6

For some people, a Mexican beach holiday is tanning in a lounge chair with a comfortable hotel and a steady supply of margaritas nearby. For others, it is a deserted beach without a soul in sight. Quintana Roo, the state on the eastern coast of the Yucatán Peninsula that is lapped by the tropical waters of the Gulf of Mexico, offers both.

For lovers of luxury and company, there is Cancún, a beehive of modern high-rise hotels, restaurants, and nightclubs. South of town, the island of Cozumel and the town of Playa del Carmen offer a little more peace and quiet. Heading further south toward the border of Belize, the towns get smaller and smaller, sometimes no bigger than a couple of cafes and a dive shop.

This stretch of coast, called the Mayan Riviera, offers some of Mexico's greatest natural beauty, both on land and underwater. For snorkelers and scuba divers, the second-largest coral reef in the world shelters a kaleidoscopic array of tropical fish, as well as the slow-swimming manatee. Salt-water lagoons are home to flamingos and pelicans, while parrots flit among the trees. Several species of sea turtles lumber onto the sand to lay their eggs. Compared to the massive pyramids at Chichén Itzá and Uxmal, the ruins at Tulum are modest in scale. But this was one of the Mayans' two seaside ceremonial cities and the only one surrounded by walls. It was also the first Mexican settlement that the Spanish explorers saw on the Mexican mainland and the only Mayan city still inhabited when the Spanish arrived in 1519. It was sufficiently impressive that they decided not to invade. Today the tourists are bolder, arriving in busloads everyday to wander among the ancient stones.

quintana roo

mexico

Along Quintana Roo's long coastline, the cooks are experts at preparing seafood fresh from the sea, including red snapper, mahi-mahi, squid, shrimp, and lobster. Sometimes they turn the catch into ceviche, fish marinated in lime juice and dressed up with avocado, tomatoes, chiles, and cilantro.

lime soup

sopa de lima

In the Yucatán, sour limes, similar to Key limes,

would flavor this soup, but the more easily obtained

Persian limes can also be used in this soup, a favorite

in the seaside towns of the Mayan Riviera.

2 quarts homemade chicken stock

1/2 cup olive oil

2 cloves garlic, minced

2 cups thinly sliced white onion

2 cups green bell peppers, seeded and thinly sliced

3 limes, thinly sliced

3 cups tomatoes, in 1/2-inch-thick slices

2 cups cooked chicken breast, hand-shredded

Salt

2 cups fresh tortilla chips

Pour chicken stock into a 4- to 6-quart pan. In a 10- to 12-inch sauté pan over medium-high heat, warm half the olive oil. Add garlic, stir, then add onion and cook until just translucent. Remove from pan with a slotted spoon and add to chicken broth.

Adding oil if necessary, sauté bell peppers in the same sauté pan until half-tender. Remove from pan with slotted spoon and add to chicken broth.

Add lime slices, tomatoes, and chicken to chicken broth mixture, and cook over medium heat until vegetables are tender. Add salt to taste, if necessary. Serve with fresh tortilla chips to add to the soup.

Serves 6

In Quintana Roo, this recipe for fish under a savory layer of vegetables, olives, and capers would most likely be made with huachinango, or red snapper, but any firm-fleshed white fish will be enhanced by this classic treatment.

1 tablespoon olive oil

5 cloves garlic, minced

2 onions, sliced

1 green pepper, seeded and sliced

2 cups peeled, seeded, and sliced tomatoes

10 capers

10 green olives

1/4 cup white wine

Salt and pepper

6 red snapper fillets

White rice

Warm olive oil in a 10- to 12-inch sauté pan over medium-high heat and add garlic. Stir for a few minutes, add onions, and cook until they are translucent. Add green pepper and cook for a few minutes; it will still be crisp. Add tomatoes, capers, olives, wine, and salt and pepper to taste. Arrange fish fillets on top of vegetables and cook for 5 to 7 minutes, until fish is done (it should be opaque but still moist looking in the center). Serve with white rice.

Serves 6

red snapper
veracruz-style

huachinango a la veracruzana

Come Friday, porteños—the residents of the port city of Buenos Aires—jump in their cars or take the little Tren de la Costa to head 27 kilometers north to a different world. This is the delta of the Paraná River, where concrete is replaced by the shimmer and flow of water and a speedboat is more useful than an automobile.

The main town is Tigre. There you can hail a boat—perhaps a wooden launch seating 100 people, or a catamaran seating 250—and tour the maze of slow-moving waterways. Or take a trip to Isla Martín Garcia, once a prison, now a nature preserve. Some fortunate Argentines have houses here. There are stately Tudor mansions as well as ramshackle wooden cabins with docks leaning precariously over the water. Many more people come for the day, to go fishing, kayaking, or waterskiing, or simply to putt-putt gently between countless islands shaded with poplars and willow trees. A wave of British immigrants in the early 1900s introduced rowing to locals. Today, everyone sculls the Tigre and the Lujan, making rowing one of the most popular watersports in Argentina.

On land, visitors stroll through the Puerto de Frutas, a former fruit market whose booths now offer handicrafts from around the world. For military buffs, there's the Museo Naval de la Nación, dedicated to the history of the Argentine navy, improbably founded by an Irishman named Guillermo Brown.

Afterward, it's time to hail a taxiboat to go to one of the many restaurants, ranging from grandly formal to scruffily casual, that line the waterways. Whether weekenders choose to be active or indolent, the delta is an essential escape from the pressures and neuroses of Buenos Aires life.

tigre

argentina

Argentines on their way to a weekend on the delta or in the pampas are apt to take along a basketful of empanadas to keep their strength up on the trip. These flaky pastries, fried or baked, are turnovers filled with a combination of hardboiled eggs, meat, chicken, cheese, olives, or raisins.

sole in lemon sauce

lenguado al limón

Fish is an appropriate choice in the restaurants that line the Paraná delta's waterways. El Gato Blanco, one of the more sophisticated and luxurious restaurants in this popular vacation spot, serves sole with a simple lemon butter.

4 8-ounce sole fillets

Salt and pepper

6 tablespoons butter

1²/₃ cups dry Champagne

2 lemons

1/2 cup sugar

2 teaspoons of cornstarch, dissolved in a little water

Preheat oven to 375°F. Season the fish fillets with salt and pepper. Arrange in a baking dish rubbed with 1 tablespoon of the butter. Pour in half the Champagne, and bake for 15 minutes.

Remove zest from lemons and slice into thin julienne strips. In a 12- to 14-inch pan over medium heat, melt remaining butter and sauté the lemon zest and sugar, stirring to combine. Add the lemon juice, and cook for 10 more minutes. Stir the cornstarch mixture and add to sauce in pan to thicken.

Arrange each fish fillet on a warmed plate and pour sauce over.

Serves 4

In Chile one is never far from La Costa. At its widest point, Chile is only 110 miles wide. And its coastline stretches for 2,600 miles along the Pacific. Pablo Neruda, one of Chile's most famous native sons, compared its rolling surf and incessant wind to a galloping horse. The Nobel Prize–winning poet was fascinated by the constant motion of the sea, and perhaps his favorite of his four houses was the one perched above the beach at Isla Negra, a coastal village south of Valparaíso. The little town is a place of pilgrimage for his adoring fans, who come to visit his house, filled with bowsprits and other nautical artifacts, and to stare at the sea as he did.

The view of the sea also defines the city of Valparaíso, which clings to hills so steep that elevators and funiculars are the most practical means of transport from the lower part of town to the upper. Although the city was founded by Spaniards in 1536, its success as a port can be credited to the British traders who settled here in the nineteenth century and gave their adopted town some of the fashions and manners of England. Novelist Isabel Allende captured the spirit of the city's nautical entrepreneurs in her saga of a Chilean family's comings and goings between Valparaíso and San Francisco. Valparaíso still has the down-at-the-heels shabbiness of a working port that at one time was heavily fortified against pirates.

For a more sanitized seaside experience, Chileans go a few kilometers north to the resort town of Viña del Mar to lounge on the beach and eat ceviche and cazuela de mariscos in one of dozens of seaside restaurants.

la costa

chile

Some of the fish and shellfish that Chile pulls from the cold currents of the Pacific Ocean are familiar to residents of the Northern Hemisphere, who will recognize the mussels, clams, scallops, shrimp, swordfish, and sole on display in the country's markets. Less familiar creatures are also popular here, notably congrio, a type of eel-like fish, giant sea urchins, and a rocklike amalgam of tiny shellfish called pibre.

conger chowder

caldillo de congrio

Conger chowder was such a favorite of Pablo Neruda that he wrote a poem about it. This recipe, from the restaurant Café del Poeta in his former home in Isla Negra, calls for congrio, a type of eel, but can be cooked with other firm-fleshed white fish.

4 cups strained fish stock, made with fish and conger heads, bay leaves, oregano, and salt

2 tablespoons vegetable oil

1 onion, thinly sliced

1 red bell pepper, seeded and thinly sliced

1 teaspoon oregano

1 teaspoon paprika

Salt

4 large pieces of conger eel, about 2 pounds total

1 clove garlic, minced

2 cups tomatoes, peeled, seeded, and chopped into 1/2-inch cubes

2 cups cooked potatoes, peeled and chopped into 1/2-inch cubes

1 cup white wine

1 cup peeled medium shrimp

2 tablespoons coarsely chopped cilantro

1 cup heavy cream

Place the fish stock in a 4- to 6-quart pot.

Warm oil in a 12- to 14-inch sauté pan over medium heat. Add onion, bell pepper, oregano, paprika, and salt to taste and cook, stirring occasionally, until vegetables are soft.

Bring stock to a simmer, add vegetable mixture, conger, garlic, tomatoes, potatoes, and wine. Cook for 5 minutes over medium heat. Add shrimp, cilantro, and cream. Cook for approximately 2 minutes or until shrimp are pink. Serve immediately.

Serves 4

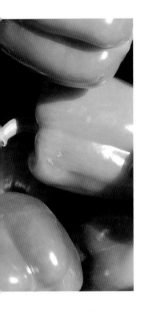

Ceviche is served all along Latin America's Pacific Coast, and there are literally hundreds of recipes. This Chilean version is one of the simplest, a perfect formula for fish fresh from the sea.

1 pound seabass fillets, cut into 1/2-inch cubes

About 1 cup lemon juice

1 medium onion, finely chopped

2 tablespoons minced cilantro

1/2 green bell pepper, seeded and finely chopped

2 tablespoons olive oil

Salt and pepper

Place fish fillets in a bowl and cover with lemon juice; you may need more lemon juice to cover the fish. Marinate until fish is "cooked"—completely white and opaque—approximately 2 hours. Add onion, cilantro, bell pepper, oil, and salt and pepper to taste. Stir gently and serve immediately.

Serves 4

seabass ceviche

ceviche de corvina

Uruapan is a busy town—a commercial center for the thriving agricultural state of Michoacán. The area produces millions of pounds of avocados annually, turning some into guacamole in local factories and exporting the rest around the world. Coffee, bananas, and macadamias also flourish in the surrounding countryside, where the combination of tropical temperatures and mountain altitudes means pineapples and fir trees grow within a few miles of each other.

The city's attractions are spread along the banks of the Cupatitzio River. One of Mexico's most accessible national parks, the Parque Nacional Eduardo Ruiz, is located almost in the middle of town. Strollers can take advantage of its shaded walkways to see the headwaters of the river and numerous cooling waterfalls.

Brightly flowered lacquered wooden boxes and trays are the stars of Uruapan's handcraft tradition. Contemporary versions are on sale at shops, while antique lacquer objects are on display at the Casa de Artesanias, a museum in La Huatapera, a sixteenth-century building built by Franciscan monks as the first hospital in the Americas. Not far away, in the village of Santa Clara de Cobre, coppersmiths have been turning out hammered vessels for hundreds of years.

Most visitors come to Uruapan for the lush, river-laced mountain scenery. They often visit the Paricutín volcano, where it is still possible to see the lava field and volcanic ash remaining from the mountain's dramatic explosion in 1943 that buried everything for miles around and left only the top of the San Juan church poking bravely out of the lava. The top of the volcano, accessible by foot or by horseback, still releases occasional puffs of steam.

uruapan

mexico

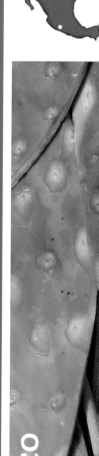

There are almost as many recipes for carnitas, a Michoacán favorite, as there are cooks. They all start with cubes of pork. Then the meat might—or might not—be marinated with citrus juices and spices before being slowly cooked in its own juices or in deep fat. It might be crisped in the oven at the end before being tucked into a roll or wrapped in a fresh tortilla.

avocado and grapefruit drink

guacamaya

Here's the Uruapan version of the smoothie—a beautifully colored breakfast in a glass. It combines the sweet-sour flavor of pink grapefruit and the delicate richness of avocado.

1 medium avocado
4 cups pink grapefruit juice
3 tablespoons sugar
3/4 cup crushed ice or ice cubes

Halve the avocado and scoop the flesh into a blender. Add juice, sugar, and ice. Blend at high speed until ice is completely crushed. Serve immediately.

Serves 2

Although many Latin American recipes depend on fresh seafood, the filling for these avocados is based on ingredients that can be kept on the shelf until the cook needs to come up with a culinary tribute to Mexico.

1/4 cup canned pimentos, chopped

1 1/4 cup oil-packed sardines, drained and chopped

2 tablespoons chopped anchovy fillets

2 tablespoons chopped capers

3 tablespoons pitted, chopped olives

1/4 cup vinegar-packed jalapeños

1 cup chopped macadamia nuts

3/4 cup olive oil

3 ripe avocados

6 romaine lettuce leaves, washed

6 hardboiled eggs, halved

6 sprigs parsley

Reserve 6 slices of pimento, and chop the rest. Combine pimentos, sardines, anchovies, capers, olives, jalapeños, macadamia nuts, and olive oil. Slice avocados in half lengthwise and remove pits. Fill each half with sardine filling. Place each avocado half on a plate garnished with a lettuce leaf, 2 hardboiled egg halves, a pimento strip, and a sprig of parsley.

Serves 6

avocados stuffed with seafood

aguacates marineros

michoacán-style trout
with avocado sauce

trucha a la michoacána con salsa de aguacate

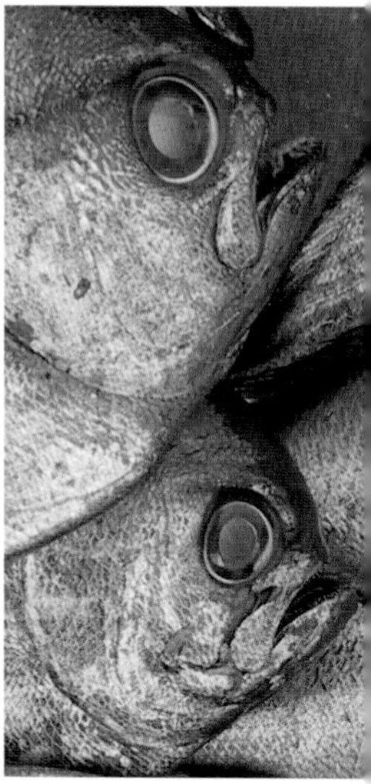

This recipe spotlights two local ingredients—trout from Michoacán's rivers and fish farms, and macadamia nuts, a recent addition to the state's rich agricultural menu.

1 avocado

6 tomatillos, husked

1 tablespoon cilantro

3 serrano chiles, seeded

1 clove garlic, peeled

1/4 cup chopped white onion

Salt

Fillets of 2 fresh trout

2/3 cup coarsely chopped macadamia nuts

2 teaspoons butter

2 teaspoons Worcestershire sauce

Halve the avocado and remove flesh. Put avocado, tomatillos, cilantro, chiles, garlic, onion, and salt to taste in a blender or food processor. Process for a few seconds, until ingredients are combined. The sauce can be chunky or smooth, depending on your taste and how long you blend it. For smoother sauce, add up to 1/4 cup water and blend longer. For chunkier sauce, blend until small pieces of tomatillo and avocado remain.

Grill or panfry the fish fillets until fish is done (it should be opaque but still moist looking in the center).

In a small sauté pan, sauté nuts in butter and Worcestershire sauce over low heat for 3 minutes.

Put a spoonful of avocado sauce on each of two warmed plates. Place the fish fillets on top and scatter the nuts over the fish. Serve with the remaining sauce on the side.

Serves 2

In multicultural Brazil, the coastal city of Salvador, capital of the state of Bahia, enshrines the nation's African heritage in its distinctive cuisine, dance, music, and religious practices. It is set among palm-shaded beaches and spectacular Baroque buildings painted in brilliant shades of blue, turquoise, pink, and ochre.

Salvador is famous for capoeira, a style of martial arts disguised as a dance. It was first developed by African slaves in order to secretly train to fight their masters. Today it is considered a form of exercise, involving kicking motions, dips, and flips performed to the sound of a slender one-stringed instrument called a berimbau.

The slaves also created mystical Afro-Brazilian religions like candomblé, merging their own deities with the Catholic saints imposed by their masters. On February 2 each year, candomblé believers dressed in white cast jewelry, flowers, perfume, and other feminine trinkets out to sea to satisfy the alleged vanity of the ocean goddess, Yemanjá. Africa also resonates through Salvador's love of percussion, particularly the vibrant sound of Oludum, a renowned group of drummers whose fame has spread far from their native city.

The city is divided into two layers connected by an elevator. In the lower city are the beaches, the ports, the crafts market in the Mercado Modelo, and the beloved church of Bonfim, popular with both Roman Catholics and candomblé practitioners. The upper city boasts sumptuous seventeenth- and eighteenth-century Baroque churches with glittering interiors embellished with gold leaf. The Pelhourino is a neighborhood of houses perched on steep and winding streets; many of them have been restored, thanks to UNESCO's interest in these examples of Portuguese colonial architecture.

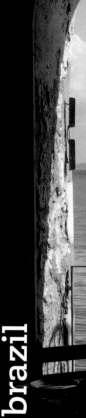

salvador

brazil

The food of Salvador has its own flavor, thanks to the use of oil from the dende palm,
an African native that has thrived in northeast Brazil's dry heat. Okra, manioc flour, peanuts,
coconut milk, malagueta chiles, and dried shrimp turn up in local dishes like vatapa, a chicken
or seafood stew; caruru de camarao, featuring dried and fresh shrimp; and acaraje, a
deep-fried bean patty embellished with hot sauce.

bahian seafood stew

moqueca

This recipe brings together some of the best elements of the cooking of Bahia state—fresh fish and shellfish flavored with lime, cumin, garlic, cilantro, hot peppers, coconut milk, and palm oil. Serve it with squares of grilled polenta for added flavor.

1/4 cup lime juice

6 cloves garlic, crushed

1/2 cup olive oil

Salt and pepper

2 pounds firm white fish, such as red snapper, cut into 1-inch cubes

2 pounds shelled shrimp

sauce:

4 tomatoes, cored and halved

2 medium onions, peeled and halved

6 cloves garlic

2 red bell peppers, halved and seeded

1/2 cup parsley

1/2 cup cilantro

1 teaspoon cumin

1/4 cup lime juice

1/2 cup olive oil

1/2 cup dende oil, or substitute peanut oil

2 onions, cut into thin slices

2 large green bell peppers, seeded and sliced

3 large tomatoes, seeded and sliced

3 cups coconut milk

1/2 cup parsley

1/2 cup cilantro leaves

Hot chiles, seeded and chopped, to taste (see note)

Salt

Hot cooked rice or grilled, sliced polenta

Note: Residents of Bahia like their food spicy, and they might put as much as 1/4 cup of searingly hot malagueta chiles into their moqueca. Those with more tender palates should use fresh chiles, such as piquin or habanero, starting with 1/2 teaspoon, and adding more as desired.

Mix together lime juice, garlic, oil, and salt and pepper to taste, stirring to dissolve salt. Marinate the seafood in this mixture for 1 hour.

To make the sauce, mix tomatoes, onions, garlic, red bell peppers, parsley, cilantro, cumin, and lime juice in a food processor; blend until smooth. Warm olive oil in a 12- to 14-inch sauté pan over medium heat. Add the tomato mixture to the pan; cook for a few minutes until it reduces. Set aside.

For the final preparation of the dish, warm dende oil in a large wok or pot over medium-high heat. Add onion and green bell peppers and cook for 5 minutes, stirring constantly. Add tomatoes and cook for 2 more minutes. Add the sauce, coconut milk, parsley, cilantro, chiles, and salt to taste and boil for 5 minutes. Add the fish and shrimp and cook for about 5 minutes more, until fish is opaque and shrimp is pink. Serve immediately with rice or polenta.

Serves 6

flan de vainilla vanilla custard

Flan originally came to Latin America from Spain, but its gentle flavor and creamy texture have made it a favorite way to end traditional meals filled with exotic ingredients and aggressive tastes.

1 1/2 cups sugar
4 cups milk
4 eggs
6 egg yolks
1 1/2 teaspoons vanilla extract

Preheat oven to 375°F. Place 3/4 cup of the sugar in a small saucepan over medium heat. Shake the pan constantly until the sugar melts and caramelizes, becoming golden brown. Pour the caramel carefully into a 1 1/2-quart mold or baking dish, turning mold so caramel coats bottom and sides. Set aside.

In a bowl, whisk together milk, eggs, egg yolks, and vanilla. Pour into the mold and cover the mold with foil. Set the mold into a larger pan, and add hot water to the pan to a depth of 1 inch. Bake in preheated oven for 1 1/2 to 2 hours or until a knife inserted into the center of the custard comes out clean.

Cool completely. To serve, place serving plate on top of the mold and invert mold. If caramel has hardened, soften it by applying a towel dipped in hot water to the bottom of the mold.

Serves 6

The city of Oaxaca de Juárez serves as the capital of the state of Oaxaca. The city's zócalo, a gracious, tree-rimmed square with a curlicued wrought-iron bandstand in the middle, is so beguiling that visitors inevitably sit under the arcades for hours. Sipping margaritas and watching the city's young people flirt with each other as they walk around the square is a favorite pastime. When the mariachi bands start playing in the early evening, the atmosphere turns magical. Life on the zócalo is only one of the many charms of an area where 2,500 years of Mexican history are on display at every turn.

About a half hour outside of town, the oldest vestiges of pre-Columbian times are the ruins of Monte Albán, the ancient ceremonial center of the Zapotec Indians, who built impressive pyramids and ball courts starting in 500 B.C. and lived here until about 800 A.D. Moving forward about 800 years, the Spanish occupation of this area is embodied by the church of Santo Domingo, whose sober exterior belies a glittering interior where sinuous carvings of leaves, branches, and saints are executed in white and gilded stucco as delicate as cake frosting.

Should history pall, Oaxaca's markets are the place to go. Country people, representing the region's 17 indigenous groups, arrive in the early dawn hours to display the ingredients for the region's complex and spicy cuisine, as well as distinctive crafts, such as carved and painted animals, textiles, rugs, and fragile green and black pottery. The Mercado de Abastos (market of goods and supplies), a kaleidoscope of sounds and smells and colors, is one of Latin America's largest and most authentic.

oaxaca

mexico

Oaxaca's cuisine is one of the most complex in Mexico, integrating Spanish and Indian influences. Chiles and chocolate are two of the many ingredients indispensable to the subtle, indefinable flavor of mole sauce. The sprawling market showcases spices, such as cinnamon and cumin, squash, black beans, banana leaves, and crispy fried grasshoppers called chapulines.

96

chiles stuffed
with picadillo

chiles rellenos de picadillo oaxaquena

Classic Oaxacan dishes like this one require patience and a long list of ingredients, but the results are worth the effort. In this recipe, large poblano chiles are stuffed with a filling made of pork or chicken enlivened by a careful balance of salty and sweet flavors, including olives, capers, cinnamon, cloves, raisins, and almonds.

picadillo stuffing:

2 pounds leg of pork, boned and cut into 2-inch cubes, or chicken breasts

3 cloves garlic, peeled

1 medium onion, cut in quarters

1 teaspoon salt

4 tablespoons vegetable oil

1 large white onion, chopped

3 pounds tomatoes, peeled, seeded, and diced

8 tomatillos, husked and diced

4 cloves garlic, peeled and chopped

15 green olives, chopped

15 capers, chopped

4 tablespoons raisins

4 ounces blanched almonds

1/2 teaspoon ground cloves

1/2 teaspoon ground cinnamon

1/2 teaspoon freshly ground pepper

2 teaspoons vinegar

1 teaspoon sugar

Salt

tomato sauce:

2 pounds tomatoes

1 thick slice white onion

2 cloves garlic, peeled

1 1/2 tablespoons vegetable oil

2 bay leaves

Salt

chiles:

12 large poblano chiles

4 eggs, separated

2 teaspoons salt

8 tablespoons flour

Vegetable oil for frying

2 tablespoons flour

Hot cooked rice

Hot tortillas

To make the picadillo stuffing, in a 6- to 8-quart stock pot, cover pork or chicken, garlic, onion, and salt with water. Simmer over low heat until the meat is very tender, about 1 1/2 hours for pork or 1/2 hour for chicken. Remove the meat from the water, reserving 3/4 cup of broth, defatted. Let the meat cool, then shred it by hand, discarding any fat.

Warm vegetable oil in a 6- to 8-quart heavy pan, and cook onion over medium heat for 3 minutes. Add tomatoes, tomatillos, garlic, olives, capers, raisins, almonds, cloves, cinnamon, and ground pepper. Simmer for 20 minutes, stirring occasionally. Add the reserved broth, shredded meat, vinegar, sugar, and salt, if necessary. Simmer for 25 minutes, until broth has cooked away.

To make the tomato sauce, place tomatoes in boiling water for a few minutes until slightly cooked. Remove from water with a slotted spoon, slip skins off, and put in a blender or food processor with onion and garlic. Blend until fairly smooth. Warm oil in a 12- to 14-inch sauté pan over medium heat; add tomato mixture, bay leaves, and salt to taste, and sauté for a few minutes until the sauce reduces slightly. Remove bay leaves.

To prepare the chiles, roast them over a gas flame, turning until they are black and blistered. Put them in a paper or plastic bag for 10 minutes. When they are cool enough to handle, peel them carefully under running water, making sure not to tear them and keeping them whole. Make a long slit down the side of each chile and very carefully remove seeds and ribs. Carefully fill each chile with 4 tablespoons of picadillo stuffing.

Beat egg whites until stiff. Add egg yolks one by one, then salt and 2 tablespoons of the flour. Place remaining flour in a shallow dish.

Pour vegetable oil into a 12- to 14-inch pan to a depth of 1/2 inch; heat on high. Coat each chile with flour, dip into egg batter, and place in the hot oil, turning gently until the batter is golden brown and thoroughly cooked.

Place two stuffed, fried chiles on each of 6 plates and cover with tomato sauce. Serve with rice and tortillas.

Serves 6

corn soup

Oaxaca's sprawling market, one of the largest and most colorful in Latin America, offers all the ingredients, including corn and zucchini blossoms, for this vegetarian soup. It's hearty enough to serve as a main course, preferably with fresh tortillas kept warm in a napkin-lined basket.

sopa de la milpa

4 poblano chiles

12 zucchini blossoms

3 tablespoons olive oil

3 cups fresh corn kernels

1 medium white onion, finely chopped

1 large clove garlic, minced

1 pound ripe tomatoes, peeled, seeded, and chopped

1 pound zucchini, cut into 1/2-inch cubes

8 ounces mushrooms, sliced

4 black peppercorns

2 whole cloves

6 cups water or chicken broth

3 sprigs epazote or cilantro, minced

Salt

8 ounces fresh cheese, such as Mexican queso fresco or fresh mozzarella, cut into 1/2-inch cubes

Prepare chiles by roasting them over a gas flame, turning until they are completely blackened. Put them in a paper or plasic bag for 10 minutes. When they are cool enough to handle, peel off the blackened skin under running water. Remove seeds, stems, and veins, and dice.

Clean zucchini blossoms, removing stems, pistils, and outer green parts.

In a large, heavy saucepan, warm olive oil over medium-high heat. Add corn kernels and sauté for 5 minutes. Add onion and sauté for 3 more minutes. Add garlic and tomatoes, lower heat, and cook for 5 more minutes, stirring occasionally. Add zucchini and mushrooms, and cook for 5 more minutes. Add peppercorns, cloves, and water or chicken broth. Add diced chiles, epazote or cilantro, and zucchini blossoms. Check for seasoning and add salt to taste.

Divide cheese among 6 bowls. Ladle soup over cheese and serve immediately.

Serves 6

Not far from the broad boulevards and spacious parks of Buenos Aires' commercial center are two neighborhoods that retain narrow streets, distinctive architecture, and a lively mixture of working-class people and artists.

In San Telmo, they are crowded into dignified but crumbling apartment buildings, built by upper-class families in the nineteenth century, and they walk along cobblestone streets that were once streams. Nearby La Boca boasts the capital's most colorful architecture—houses that are a patchwork of bright colors and inexpensive materials, including sheets of corrugated iron. This was once the home of Basque and Italian immigrants, who settled along the waterway called the Riachuelo and built their homes of shipbuilding scraps. Today, the neighborhood's most picturesque street, the Caminito, is still a place to find inexpensive Italian meals of pizza and pasta.

Both neighborhoods boast art galleries, outdoor cafes, antique shops, and flea markets. But they are above all places to sample tango, the dance born in the local brothels of the loneliness of recent immigrants. Here, the relationship of pimp and prostitute is put to rhythms borrowed from Africa and the Argentine hinterland, played on a version of the German accordion. The tango was considered impossibly lower class, even obscene, by respectable Argentines, until the French discovered it in the early twentieth century. Today, its comeback is obvious in La Boca and San Telmo, where crowds ranging in age from children to dignified grandmothers stare intently at couples dancing sensuously in the streets. Aspiring dancers, not quite ready for the murmured critiques of the public, can study tango at the area's tango schools.

san telmo

argentina

Although Argentina stretches from the steamy jungles on its northern border with Brazil to the icy plains of southern Patagonia, it is primarily a temperate country, with a cuisine short on the aggressive chile peppers and tropical fruits of the rest of South America. It's not surprising that culinary students in Buenos Aires spend a lot of time studying the subtleties of French cooking and that Buenos Aires prides itself on its stylish French restaurants.

duck confit sandwich

sandwich de confit de pato

This is a very fancy sandwich indeed, designed not as a casual snack, but as an imaginative first course, or as an accompaniment to grilled duck breast in one of the many restaurants in Buenos Aires where the ingredients are local but the techniques are French. It requires patience, but the combination of rich, thyme-scented duck meat and intensely sweet fruit is exceptional.

4 duck legs

4 tablespoons coarse salt

4 sprigs thyme

2 cups liquefied duck fat

3 ripe plums

1/2 cup sugar

1 tablespoon anise

8 2-inch squares of warm, cooked puff pastry

Sprinkle duck legs with salt, add thyme, and refrigerate for several hours. Next, place duck in a 2- to 4-quart heavy saucepan, cover with duck fat, and simmer, covered with a lid, over very low heat for 3 to 4 hours, until the meat falls from the bones. Remove meat from bones and reserve.

Pit and slice plums and place in a 1 1/2- to 2-quart saucepan. Add sugar and anise and cover with 4 cups water. Cook over very low heat for 2 to 3 hours, until the plums become a thick sauce.

Pile duck meat on puff pastry, layer with plum sauce, top with another square of puff pastry, and serve immediately.

Serves 4

For centuries, Cuernavaca has been the favored destination of Mexico City residents escaping the capital's traffic, noise, and crowds. Moctezuma II, emperor of the Aztecs, came here. So did Hernán Cortés, the great conquistador, and the doomed Emperor Maximilian and his wife Carlota. Mexican presidents, American movie stars, moneyed expatriates, artists, and writers followed in their footsteps, attracted by Cuernavaca's springlike climate and verdant mountain scenery.

Most of the city's luxurious haciendas and terraced gardens are tucked away from the casual visitor. That graffiti-scrawled garage door or pock-marked adobe wall may hide acres of garden splashing with fountains and bright with bougainvillea and jacaranda. But a tourist can get a glimpse of the good life by visiting some of the city's museums and the haciendas that have been turned into hotels and sophisticated restaurants. Close to the zócalo, the Brady Museum is the former residence of an American art connoisseur, the late Robert Brady, who collected primitive and religious art from around the world, as well as works of contemporary Mexican artists like Rufino Tamayo and Frida Kahlo. Farther from the center of town, the Hacienda de Cortés, once the home of Martín Cortés and later a barracks for Emiliano Zapata's revolutionary troops, now offers the peaceful opportunity to dine among romantic courtyards and tile-roofed buildings.

It's not all idle luxury in Cuernavaca. Thousands of tourists come here each year to study Spanish at one of the town's dozens of schools. They're the ones earnestly frowning as they attempt to use their best subjunctives to buy a pair of earrings at the outdoor silver market, in the shadow of Cortés's palace near the center of town.

cuernavaca

mexico

Cuernavaca, a favorite weekend destination for sophisticated residents of Mexico City, boasts a wide variety of restaurants, ranging from informal cantinas to upscale establishments reinterpreting classical recipes and familiar ingredients. In either case, a view of a beautifully maintained tropical garden is almost always part of the Cuernavaca dining experience.

coconut ice cream
with two sauces

Here is a dessert as beautiful to look at as it is delicious to eat.

Serve it on plain white or solid black plates for a particularly dramatic effect. Bottled hibiscus syrup, labeled as jarabe de jamaica, can be obtained in Latin American specialty groceries.

helado de coco
con dos salsas

coconut ice cream:

1 1/2 cups whole milk

1/2 cup Crema Mexicana or heavy cream

5 egg yolks

1/2 cup superfine sugar

2 teaspoons vanilla extract

1/2 cup thick unsweetened coconut cream

1/3 cup dried unsweetened shredded coconut

mango sauce:

2 medium ripe mangos

1 tablespoon dark rum

1 to 2 tablespoons superfine sugar (or to taste)

blackberry sauce:

3/4 cup hibiscus flowers (optional)

1/2 cup sugar

1 pint ripe blackberries

Fresh mint (optional)

To make the ice cream, bring milk and Crema Mexican or cream to a simmer in a heavy saucepan. Remove from heat and let cool slightly. Beat egg yolks and sugar in a medium bowl until they are light and foamy. Slowly stir in warm milk and cream. Return mixture to saucepan and cook over medium heat, stirring constantly with a wooden spoon until the mixture thickens to coat the spoon. Stir in vanilla, coconut cream, and shredded coconut. Put a layer of plastic wrap directly on the liquid and chill in the refrigerator.

When the custard is cold, freeze in an ice cream maker according to manufacturer's instructions. Pour the ice cream into a loaf pan or mold, lined with plastic wrap, and freeze.

Peel mangos and remove flesh. Purée the flesh and rum in a blender or food processor. Pass through a sieve and chill until ready to use. If necessary, add sugar and a little water so the mixture has a thick pouring consistency.

If you are using the hibiscus flowers, boil them in 2 cups of water with the sugar, until the liquid has been reduced by half. Strain.

Purée blackberries in a food processor or blender, pass them through a sieve to remove seeds, and add 2 tablespoons of the hibiscus syrup or sugar to taste. Chill.

To serve, spoon mango syrup on one side of a dessert plate and blackberry syrup on the other. Place a slice of ice cream in the center and garnish with mint, if desired.

Serves 6 to 8

nopal salad

ensalada de nopalitos

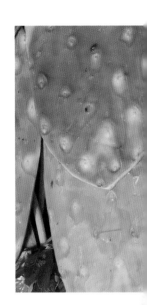

On Mexico's high plateau, cactus seems to grow everywhere, and its edible properties have been extensively explored by native cooks. In this recipe, tomatillo husks or baking soda reduce the gelatinous texture of nopal cactus paddles, leaving the delicate flesh ready for the addition of radishes, onion, cilantro, and lime juice.

8 to 10 medium-sized nopal cactus paddles, or 3 cups canned nopal

Husks of 10 tomatillos or 1/4 teaspoon baking soda

3 cloves garlic

1/4 large white onion

Pinch of salt

1/2 cup chopped red radishes

1/2 cup chopped green onion

1/4 cup minced cilantro

1 serrano chile, seeded and minced

1/4 teaspoon ground cumin

3 tablespoons lime juice

Salt and freshly ground pepper

Note: The paddles of the nopal cactus exude a slippery substance when cooked. Adding tomatillo husks or a bit of baking soda during the cooking process will eliminate this. It is also possible to use canned nopal, which must be rinsed thoroughly.

Wearing heavy gloves, clean the cactus paddles by slicing off the spines and scraping down the bumps, but do not peel entirely. Cut off tough edges, then slice the paddles into 1/4-inch strips. Boil 6 to 8 quarts of water in an 8- to 10-quart stock pot. Add nopal slices, tomatillo husks or baking soda, garlic, onion, and salt to boiling water and cook for 10 to 12 minutes, until the nopal is soft and olive green in color. Drain nopal and discard garlic, onion, and husks. Cool.

In a large bowl, mix nopal slices with radishes, green onion, cilantro, serrano chile, cumin, lime juice, and salt and pepper to taste. Chill well before serving.

Serves 6

Mexico introduced corn to the first European explorers, but Europe returned the favor by bringing rice, the bounty of the Orient, to the New World. Mexican cooks are masters at enhancing the basic grain with chicken broth, tomatoes, vegetables, and typical Mexican herbs and spices, ending up with a dish rich and flavorful enough to be served as a separate course.

1 1/2 cups long-grain rice

4 Roma tomatoes, cored

1 to 2 cloves garlic, peeled

3 cups chicken stock, or water with 1 chicken bouillon cube

2 to 3 tablespoons vegetable oil

3/4 cup finely chopped carrot

1/3 cup finely chopped white onion

1/3 cup fresh or frozen peas

Salt

Rinse rice in hot water. Drain in a colander and let dry for a few minutes.

Place tomatoes, garlic, and stock or water with bouillon cube in a blender and liquefy.

Warm vegetable oil in a wide pan (an earthenware cazuela, if possible) over medium heat. Add carrot and onion, and cook for 5 minutes. Add rice and cook, stirring constantly, until the grains become translucent and start to turn golden.

Strain the tomato mixture onto the rice. Stir briefly and add peas. Cover and cook over low heat until water is absorbed and small holes appear in the surface of the rice, about 20 minutes. Fluff the rice with a fork, season with salt to taste, and serve.

Serves 6

mexican rice

las campanas arroz mexicana

The long history of San Juan, the oldest city in the Western hemisphere, is easy to imagine in the part of the capital known as Old San Juan. Here the streets are narrow and cobbled, fountains play in the plazas, and Spanish colonial buildings have been carefully restored and painted in luscious pastel colors. Much of the area is still enclosed by 40-foot walls built in the seventeenth century. Art galleries, antique shops, and clothing boutiques compete for the attention of cruise ship passengers wandering through the neighborhood.

The most impressive historical site in the city is the Castillo del Morro, a massive fortress overlooking the entrance to San Juan Bay. The fort's heavy walls and round towers, facing out toward the Atlantic Ocean, are a vivid symbol of the Spaniards' determination to protect their lucrative New World empire. Numerous invaders, including Sir Francis Drake, tried in vain to take it over, but it was not until 1898 that El Morro finally fell to the Americans. Its strategic position and its dungeons and barracks appeal especially to military history buffs, but everyone can enjoy the spectacular ocean and city views from El Morro's ramparts.

Of course, San Juan is also a modern city of one million people, and many visitors come here not for the past but for contemporary pleasures like the beaches at Condado and Isla Verde, salsa dancing at the discos, and drinking Puerto Rico's signature drink, the rich and frothy Piña Colada.

san juan

puerto rico

Puerto Rico may be only a medium-sized island, but it has a cuisine complex and varied enough for a large country—with a vocabulary to match. Bacalaitos (cod fritters), asopaos (soupy stews made of chicken, seafood, and vegetables), adobo (a spicy rub for meat and poultry), and sofrito (the sautéed onion, pepper, tomato, and spices that are the first step of many dishes) are not only words but recipes worth learning.

mofongo with shrimp

mofongo con camarones

Anyone doubting that Puerto Rico has a unique cuisine need only try mofongo, cooked green plantains mashed in a mortar with garlic and pork fat.

mofongo:

2 green plantains

About 1 quart of vegetable oil for deep-fat frying

1/2 cup chicharrón (crisp-fried pork skin), chopped crisp bacon, or lean chopped ham

1 tablespoon minced garlic

2 tablespoons olive oil

sofrito:

2 tablespoons olive oil

1 green bell pepper, seeded, deribbed, and diced

1 onion, finely chopped

1 tablespoon minced garlic

1 cup minced cilantro

Salt and pepper

1 tablespoon olive oil

1/2 cup chopped red bell pepper

1 cup homemade tomato sauce

1 tablespoon capers

1 tablespoon finely chopped olives

2 tablespoons minced cilantro

1 tablespoon minced garlic

2 tablespoons olive oil

10 large shrimp, peeled

1/4 cup white wine

To make mofongo, peel plantains and cut into 2-inch-thick slices. Fry plantains in very hot oil in a large saucepan or deep fat fryer for 10 minutes. Remove with a slotted spoon and transfer to a very large mortar and pestle; mash the plantains with the chicharrón, bacon, or ham; minced garlic; and olive oil. Make a deep dent in the mixture, so that it forms a bowl in the mortar. Keep warm.

To make the sofrito, warm olive oil in a 10- to 12-inch sauté pan over medium-high heat and add green bell pepper, onion, and garlic. Cook until soft, about 5 minutes, then add cilantro and salt and pepper to taste. Remove mixture from pan and set aside.

Warm olive oil in an 8-inch sauté pan over medium-high heat, add red bell pepper and cook, stirring occasionally, until soft, about 5 minutes. Set aside.

In a 1- to 1 1/2-quart saucepan over medium heat, combine tomato sauce, capers, olives, and cilantro. Set aside.

In a 12- to 14-inch sauté pan over medium-high heat, sauté garlic in olive oil. Stir, then add shrimp. Add sofrito, followed by red bell pepper, and stir for a minute. Then add white wine and tomato sauce mixture, and cook until shrimp are just cooked and ingredients are blended. Pour the shrimp mixture into the mortar lined with the mofongo.

Serves 2

Guanajuato's history is rich—literally. This delightful city in the mountains of central Mexico grew and prospered because of its mines, which at one time were the world's primary source of silver. As the money poured in, the city spread its candy-colored buildings along curving, cobblestone streets that cling to the sides of a narrow ravine. Guanajuato is also an icon of the War of Independence, thanks to the rebels' victorious siege of the Alhóndiga de Granadita, an imposing grain storehouse where Spanish troops had holed up.

But Guanajuato is more than a charming souvenir of past glories, and not just because it's the hometown of Mexico's charismatic political figure, Vicente Fox. The city thrives in the present tense, with the energy of a youthful population attracted to the local university, known for its observatory and its tradition of singing groups that perform in the streets. Students, residents, and tourists crowd happily into one of Mexico's smallest and most charming town squares, the Jardín de la Unión, actually a narrow triangle lined with tree-shaded cafes. Nearby, the Teatro Juárez, a confection of neoclassical façade and florid Moorish interior, offers a glittering setting for performances during the Cervantino, the city's annual arts festival commemorating Spanish author Miguel Cervantes.

The town's tourist attractions are unusual, even quirky. Energetic tourists can climb up the narrow streets to the monument to El Pipila, the young man who sacrificed himself to burn the Spaniards out of the Alhóndiga. Or they can take an elevator deep into the ground to see mining activities at La Valenciana, once the world's most productive silver mines. The house of painter Diego Rivera is open to the public, as is the Mummy Museum, a curiously popular display of mummified corpses.

guanajuato

mexico

Heaps of bananas, mangos, avocados, and cherimoyas, colorfully wrapped chocolate, stacks of tortillas, and all the other elements of classic central Mexican cuisine get a spectacular setting in the natural light that pours through the windows of the Mercado Hidalgo, a former train station constructed in iron and glass. Visitors should also take a long look at the displays of candy, a Guanajuato specialty whose myriad forms include tiny sugared mummies, a tribute to the city's Mummy Museum.

miners' enchiladas

enchiladas mineras

This recipe, a tribute to the miners who extracted silver and gold from Guanajuato's hillsides, uses easily available ingredients—chicken, carrots, and potatoes—wrapped in tortillas softened briefly in a sauce flavored with the smoky taste of ancho chiles.

adobo sauce:

5 ounces dried ancho chiles

1 white onion, coarsely chopped

6 cloves garlic, peeled

1 1/2 teaspoons powdered chicken bouillon

1 1/2 teaspoons sugar

2 teaspoons salt

1 1/2 teaspoons dried oregano

6 medium potatoes, peeled and cut into 1-inch cubes

6 carrots, peeled and cut into 1-inch sections

3- to 4-pounds chicken pieces, meat deboned and cut into 1-inch cubes

About 1 tablespoon vegetable oil

6 large corn tortillas

2 cups shredded mild cheese, such as queso fresco, Manchego, or Monterey Jack

for garnish:

Lettuce

Sliced tomatoes

Pickled green chiles

To make the adobo sauce, in a 1-quart saucepan over medium heat, cook the chiles, onion, garlic, powdered chicken bouillon, sugar, salt, and oregano in 1 cup water. When chiles are soft, pour everything into a blender or food processor. Process until smooth, then strain into a bowl, pressing down on the vegetables with the back of a wooden spoon.

Cook potatoes and carrots in boiling water until tender when pierced. Either on a griddle or in a sauté pan over medium heat, warm oil and cook chicken until just done (no longer pink in center and juices run clear). Add cooked carrots and potatoes to griddle or sauté pan, and cook until vegetables are lightly browned, about 5 minutes.

Dip tortillas in adobo sauce. Heat for 10 seconds on each side on griddle or in sauté pan. Place 1/3 cup cheese on each tortilla, heat briefly until cheese melts, and roll up. Serve tortillas with chicken, potatoes, and carrots on the side, garnished with lettuce, sliced tomatoes, and pickled chiles.

Serves 6

avocado sauce

guacamole

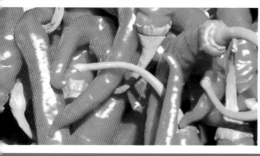

There may be hundreds of secret recipes for Mexico's favorite salsa, the irresistible guacamole, but there's agreement that the texture should be chunky, not blender smooth. Here, the soft avocados are gently mashed with two spoons before the onion, tomato, serrano chile, cilantro, and a generous squeeze of lime are added.

3 ripe avocados

1 cup tomatoes, peeled, seeded, and finely chopped

1 cup finely chopped white onion

2 tablespoons minced cilantro

1 tablespoon minced serrano chile

2 tablespoons fresh lime juice, or to taste

Salt

Tortilla chips

Halve the avocados and scoop the flesh into a bowl. Mash using two spoons. Add the tomatoes, onion, cilantro, and chile. Stir in lime juice and salt to taste. Serve with tortilla chips.

Serves 6

Simultaneously Gold Rush town and architectural museum, with a little political rebellion thrown in for flavor, Ouro Prêto brings alive the turbulent history of Brazil's interior, the rugged landscapes far from Rio's beaches and São Paolo's skyscrapers.

Ouro Prêto, meaning black gold, earned its name in 1690 when a visitor picked up a black rock that turned out to be laced with gold. The rush was on, and the town sprang up. Portuguese goldseekers, and the Jesuit priests that followed them, were responsible for the town's astonishing array of Baroque and Rococo churches, painted delicious colors outside and decorated with hundreds of kilos of gold inside. Sculptor Antonio Francisco Lisboa, known as the Aleijadinho, the little cripple, strapped hammer and chisel to his paralyzed hands to create powerfully humanistic statues for some of the churches. Today 13 of these jewel boxes have been preserved and designated world cultural monuments by UNESCO.

In 1792 Ouro Prêto was also the birthplace of an ill-fated movement to declare Brazil's independence from the Portuguese and their heavy taxes. Spies reported the planned uprising, and its leader, known as Tiradentes, was executed on the town square that now bears his name.

Eventually the gold was depleted, and the state capital moved north to Belo Horizonte, leaving Ouro Prêto more picturesque than powerful. Fortunately, the surrounding mountains offered other mineral riches, in the form of precious and semi-precious stones and soapstone. These have provided both an economic base and an incentive for skilled craftsmanship. Ouro Prêto is a university town and a cultural center with five museums and a lively arts festival every July.

ouro prêto

brazil

Brazil is a vast country and its cuisine is based on Portuguese, African, and Indian styles of cooking. One of the most popular regional specialties comes from Ouro Prêto, a city known for cheese-making as well as Baroque churches. Pão de Queijo is a puff of cheese-filled dough comparable to the French gougère, except that in Brazil, it's made with manioc flour and a soft, mild-flavored white cheese called queijo minas.

124

chicken
with a chiffonade of greens

pollo ora pro nobis

If you were making this in Brazil, you would have access to a green called ora pro nobis, a protein-rich green native to the Ouro Prêto region. If you can't find it, substitute a chiffonade of Swiss chard, collard greens, or kale, sautéed in olive oil with a little garlic.

1/4 cup plus 1 tablespoon vegetable oil

1 3- to 4-pound chicken, cut into 8 pieces

3 tablespoons flour

2 medium onions, chopped

5 cloves garlic, peeled and crushed in a mortar with 2 teaspoons salt

1 cup minced cilantro

1/4 cup chopped green onions

1 28-ounce can whole tomatoes, drained and coarsely chopped

2 tablespoons tomato paste

3 bay leaves

8 ounces ora pro nobis, washed, dried, and finely sliced, or substitute kale, collard greens, or Swiss chard

Salt and pepper

Hot cooked polenta or boiled manioc

In a heavy, 12- to 14-inch sauté pan over medium-high heat, warm 1/4 cup of the oil and brown chicken pieces. Remove them to a plate and sprinkle them with flour.

In the same pan, sauté onions until soft, stir in garlic, and cook for 3 more minutes. Then add cilantro, green onions, tomatoes, and tomato paste. Return the chicken to the pan, stirring to coat each piece with sauce. Add bay leaves and 2 cups water to cover, reduce heat to low, cover with a lid, and cook for 1 hour. Remove the chicken pieces and set aside. Remove the bay leaves and reserve the sauce. Remove the chicken from the bones.

In a 12- to 14-inch sauté pan, warm 1 tablespoon of the vegetable oil over medium-high heat and sauté greens for 2 minutes, stirring often. Add the chicken and the sauce, add salt and pepper to taste, and reheat over medium heat, stirring occasionally.

Serve immediately with polenta or manioc.

Serves 6

cowboy beans
minas gerais–style

Think Gold Rush, think men intent on exploring Brazil's inland

mountains in search of quick fortune. This recipe—a complete

meal on a plate—is the kind of food they would have enjoyed.

feijoa tropeiro

1/2 cup dried kidney beans

3 tablespoons salt

1 bay leaf

1 onion, halved

4 ounces lean bacon, cut cross-wise into 1/2-inch strips

About 5 tablespoons olive oil

4 eggs

3 cloves garlic, minced

3 medium onions, chopped

11/2 cups manioc flour

2 yellow bell peppers, seeded and cut into 1/2-inch cubes

2 red bell peppers, seeded and cut into 1/2-inch cubes

Salt and black pepper

5 to 6 drops malagueta chile sauce, or substitute any other hot sauce

6 to 8 scallions, chopped

1/2 cup minced parsley

Place beans in a bowl and fill bowl with water. Soak the beans overnight. The next day, drain them and place them in a large pot with 4 cups of water, salt, bay leaf, and onion. Bring to a boil, reduce heat and let simmer until the beans are tender, about 40 minutes. Drain and rinse beans, discarding bay leaf and onion.

In a 12- to 14-inch sauté pan, fry the bacon over medium heat until crisp. Remove from pan and drain on paper towels. Discard all but 1 tablespoon of the bacon fat in the pan and add 1 tablespoon of the olive oil. Beat the eggs and add to the pan, cooking them over medium heat for about 3 minutes, turning and tilting the pan as if you were making an omelet. Slide the cooked egg out of the pan and slice into 1-inch squares.

Add 1 tablespoon of the olive oil to the same pan. Over medium heat, sauté garlic for 2 minutes. Add chopped onions and sauté until golden brown, stirring occasionally. Add the onions and garlic to the beans.

Add remaining 3 tablespoons of the olive oil to the sauté pan. Add manioc flour and cook over medium heat, scraping up any residue in the pan, for 5 minutes, until the manioc turns golden.

In a large, heavy pan, combine beans, bacon, cooked egg, and manioc. Stir over medium heat for 3 minutes, shaking the pan gently to combine the ingredients. Add the bell peppers and salt and black pepper to taste and a few drops of pepper sauce. If the mixture seems dry, add a little olive oil.

Place the beans in a serving dish, and garnish with chopped scallions and minced parsley.

Serves 8

Ponce, Puerto Rico's second largest city, has been the beneficiary of a lavish restoration project that has polished many of its architectural gems. Although some of these are Spanish colonial in style, Ponce also offers up the neoclassical columns of the Teatro La Perla, the Municipal Fire House's Victorian curlicues, and the Moorish detailing of the Casa Salazar, a historical museum. Pink marble, wrought iron balconies, and gas lamps are oft-repeated details seen in Ponce's historical center.

Ponce is also a living and lively cultural center, where music and art are always on display. The Caribbean's largest museum of contemporary art is housed in a handsome building by Edward Durell Stone. People also come to Ponce from all over the island to buy vejigantes, huge, brightly painted papier-mache masks that freely combine human and animal features. Representing different characters, both saints and sinners, the masks are an essential element of Carnival celebrations.

Puerto Rico's music is played on instruments like a 10-stringed guitar called a cuatro, hollow gourds called guiros, tree-trunk drums, and maracas. Many of these unusual instruments are on display in the Museum of Puerto Rican Music. Ponce is also a showplace for performances of bomba y plena, two different forms of dance music that are generally presented in tandem. The first is purely African in inspiration, played on small and large drums. The plena, played on guitars, gourds, and tambourines, blends the sounds of Spain, Africa, and Puerto Rico's indigenous Taino Indians.

ponce

puerto rico

Puerto Rico's traditional cuisine has been rightly accused of being heavy and full of animal fat, but contemporary health concerns are inspiring chefs to lighten up a bit. They bake instead of fry, use olive oil rather than lard, and let the natural flavors of the island's incredible bounty of fresh fish, root vegetables, and tropical fruits shine through. Low-fat sauces sparkle with the intense flavors of garlic, capers, olives, ginger, and cilantro.

red snapper fillet
stuffed with lobster and shrimp

filete de huachinango con mariscos

Ultra-fresh seafood, snatched from the sparkling sea that surrounds Puerto Rico, needs little embellishment. In this simple, elegant treatment, Chef Luis Torres of Ponce combines snapper with lobster and shrimp, cooked in a bit of butter and white wine with a crisp touch of barely tender onion and pepper.

1 8- to 10-ounce red snapper fillet

Salt and pepper

3 ounces cooked lobster meat, sliced

4 medium cooked shrimp, shelled and sliced in half

3 tablespoons butter

1/4 cup dry white wine

1/2 small white onion, thinly sliced

1/2 green bell pepper, seeded and thinly sliced

Parsley for garnish

Butterfly the fish fillet by slicing it almost through horizontally. Season with salt and pepper to taste. Place the lobster and shrimp on one half of the fillet and fold the other half over. In an 8- to 10-inch sauté pan, melt butter over medium heat and add wine. Place stuffed fillet in pan, and cook, covered, for 3 minutes on one side. Turn the fish, and cover with the sliced onion and pepper. Cook, covered with a lid, for 2 more minutes. Serve immediately, garnished with parsley.

Serves 2

fried plantains

tostones

In Puerto Rico and in much of the Caribbean and Central America, the local equivalent of the potato chip is the plantain chip, fried, flattened, and refried to a dark brown crisp. Note that green plantains are not sweet.

2 cups corn oil

3 green plantains, peeled and cut into 1-inch-thick diagonal slices

In a deep 10- to 12-inch frying pan or a 2- to 3-quart saucepan, heat the oil until it is very hot but not smoking, about 375°F. Carefully put the plantain slices into the oil (you may want to use a long-handled slotted spoon) and fry, stirring occasionally, until they are golden brown, about 3 to 4 minutes. Remove the plantains with a slotted spoon, but maintain the oil temperature. When the plantains are cool enough to handle, place each slice between two pieces of wax paper, and, with a rolling pin, flatten to a thickness of 1/4 inch. Return the plantains to the hot oil and fry until dark brown, about 2 to 3 minutes. Remove from oil and drain on paper towels. Serve hot.

Serves 6

Mérida, principal city of the Yucatán Peninsula, was founded in 1542 on the site of a Mayan town. Today, it marches—or strolls—through life at its own leisurely pace, epitomized by the horses and buggies that clop slowly around the laurel-shrouded Plaza Mayor. Or perhaps a better symbol of the city's atmosphere of tropical leisure is the ubiquitous hammock, a local specialty crafted of Yucatecan materials, particularly sisal and cotton. In any case, there's no reason to hurry in the steamy Caribbean air. Better to find a seat on the plaza on a Sunday afternoon, when brass and marimba bands burst into song.

The tempo may be slow, but Mérida is a sophisticated city, influenced by waves of immigrants—Lebanese and French, among others—who followed the Spaniards. The newcomers settled here to trade and to grow henequen and sisal, sturdy fibers stripped from the agave plant. The immigrants and the native Mayans coexisted in relative isolation from the rest of Mexico, whose high plateaus were a world away from the peninsula's flat expanses lapped by the sea. It was not until the middle of the last century that a decent road connected the capital to the Yucatán.

For many people, Mérida is the jumping-off spot for the imposing Mayan ceremonial cities of Uxmal and Chichén Itzá, but the city has its own attractions, including fine nineteenth-century mansions, an interesting anthropology museum, and one of the least politically correct sculptures around, depicting conquistadores with their feet planted firmly on the heads of the—presumably Mayan—conquered.

mérida

mexico

Isolated from the rest of Mexico by climate and altitude, the Yucatán produced its own clothing—the crisp white man's shirt called a guayabera and the flower-embroidered huipil for women—and its own cuisine. Black beans, banana leaves, bitter oranges, pumpkin seeds, and wild turkey are part of the cuisine that many consider Mexico's best.

pork in banana leaf

cochinita pibil

Cochinita pibil combines both classical Yucatecan ingredients, including banana leaves and achiote paste, and a local technique of cooking the pork underground on a slow fire. A barbecue or oven can be substituted.

salsa:

2 cups finely chopped red onion

2 cups sour orange juice or white vinegar

1 teaspoon salt

1 habanero chile, minced

6 1/2 pounds pork leg or loin

1 tablespoon minced garlic

1 teaspoon salt

1/2 teaspoon freshly ground pepper

1/2 cup achiote paste

2 cups sour orange juice or white vinegar

2 banana leaves

1 teaspoon dried oregano

1 pound refried black beans

Corn tortillas

Make the salsa several hours before serving the cochinita pibil. To eliminate the strong flavor of the chopped onion, plunge it into a pot of boiling water for a few seconds, then strain and rinse in cold water. Place the chopped onion in a bowl and add orange juice or vinegar, salt, and habanero chile. Chill.

Cut pork into 2-inch cubes and season with garlic, salt, and pepper. Dissolve achiote paste in orange juice or vinegar; strain and pour over pork. Marinate for at least 1 hour.

To cook the pork, place a banana leaf in the bottom of a heavy casserole with a tight-fitting lid. Add pork, marinade, and oregano. Cover with second banana leaf. Cover with lid, using aluminum foil to seal. Bake at 325°F for about 2 hours, until meat is very tender. Serve with refried beans, tortillas, and salsa.

Serves 8

Although oregano can be substituted for epazote in this recipe for rolled chicken tacos, it is worth checking out Latin American markets for the real thing, which gives an authentic flavor of Mexico to this recipe.

tomato sauce:

1 pound plum tomatoes, halved and seeded

1/3 cup white onion

1 red bell pepper, halved and seeded

2 tablespoons vegetable oil

1 sprig of epazote or oregano

1 chicken bouillon cube

Salt

filling:

1 pound boned chicken breast

Salt and pepper

1 tablespoon soy sauce

1 teaspoon minced garlic

16 4-inch corn tortillas

Vegetable oil for deep frying

1/2 cup grated Manchego or Edam cheese

To make tomato sauce, put tomatoes, onion, pepper, and 2 tablespoons of water in a blender or food processor and process until smooth. Warm oil in a 10- to 12-inch sauté pan over medium heat, and add tomato mixture, epazote or oregano, bouillon cube, and salt to taste. Cook, stirring frequently, for about 10 minutes, until sauce has thickened slightly.

Meanwhile, season chicken breast with salt and pepper to taste, soy sauce, and garlic. Cook on a grill until done (no longer pink in center and juices run clear). Remove and shred by hand.

Place a spoonful of chicken on each tortilla, roll up, and fasten with a toothpick. Heat oil in a deep fat fryer. Fry filled tortillas until golden brown and drain on paper towels. Serve immediately, covered with tomato sauce and sprinkled with grated cheese.

Serves 8

rolled chicken tacos

codzitos

cream of cilantro soup

crema de cilantro

Surprising but true, cilantro is not native to Mexico. Nevertheless, it has become an indispensable ingredient in many of the country's recipes, but nowhere is it more intensely itself than in this soup.

3 tablespoons butter

3 stalks celery, coarsely chopped

1 white onion, chopped

1 green bell pepper, seeded and coarsely chopped

2 cloves garlic, coarsely chopped

1 leek, white part only, coarsely chopped

3 tablespoons flour

2 quarts milk

3 bay leaves

3 bunches cilantro

2 chicken bouillon cubes

Salt and pepper

Croutons

Melt butter in a large saucepan and cook celery, onion, bell pepper, garlic, and leek over medium heat until vegetables are soft. Add flour and stir for 1 minute. Add 1 quart of the milk and bay leaves.

Remove coarse stems from cilantro and discard. Purée cilantro leaves in a food processor or blender. Add the remaining 1 quart of milk and stir into the vegetables in the large saucepan. Crumble bouillon cubes into the soup, and heat to a simmer, stirring occasionally. Strain the soup before serving, season with salt and pepper to taste, and sprinkle croutons on top.

Serves 8

There may be a few hardworking Puritans in Rio de Janeiro, but they're hard to find in this city that seems to be on perpetual vacation. The city's beaches—Copacabana, Ipanema, and others less well known—play the role of town square. Groups of friends meet regularly at the same spots on the sand almost every day. They play footvolley, Brazil's cross between soccer and volleyball, sunbathe, or talk business and gossip.

Cariocas, as the city's residents are called, dress the part of people on holiday. Beach fashion, even the barely visible string bikini called fio dental (dental floss) is also street fashion, ties and jackets are rarely required, even in the city's most fashionable restaurants, and the whole city goes mad for festive costumes during Carnival.

The intoxicating rhythms of samba and bossa nova are everywhere, and samba schools act as social clubs that prepare all year for Carnival, when they compete for honors in the Sambódromo, an open-air arena designed especially for these contests.

Rio also has a vibrant visual arts scene, much of it centered in the Bohemian neighborhood of Santa Teresa, accessible by a tram that climbs to the top of the ridge. This was a posh neighborhood in the nineteenth century, but now its winding cobblestone streets and worn-at-the-heels mansions are home to artists, bistros, and congenial cafes offering the tiny cups of strong Brazilian coffee called cafezinhos. The cinema industry is also important in Rio; the poignant drama called *Central Station* earned an Oscar nomination for revealing the harsher realities of life in this city that works so hard at having fun.

rio de janeiro

brazil

One of the culinary traditions of Rio de Janeiro is eating feijoada for lunch on Saturday, either at home or in a restaurant. Feijoada, considered the national dish of Brazil, is a magnificent array of dried, salted, and fresh meats, served with black beans, rice, shredded kale, manioc meal, sliced oranges, and hot sauce. It started out as slave food but is now served at all levels of society.

black beans
with fresh and cured meat

feijoada

If it's Saturday, it's time for feijoada, if only because the average cook will need all morning to prepare this array of fresh, smoked, and salted meat with all its traditional accompaniments. There are almost as many recipes for feijoada as there are Brazilians, so feel free to substitute, add to, or subtract from the list of meats here. Beef tongue, a pig's foot, beef chuck roast, Portuguese linguiça sausage, Italian sausage, ham hocks, corned beef, breast of pork, and salt pork are possible additions. If you want real authenticity, toss in a couple of pig's ears and a pig's tail.

3 pounds black beans

8 ounces smoked bacon, in one piece

2 bay leaves

1 pound beef jerky

8 ounces salted pork loin or Canadian bacon

2 pound spareribs, corned or smoked if possible

2 pounds sausages of various types, such as bratwurst and chorizo

2 pounds fresh pork loin

1/4 cup bottled red peppers, such as hot cherry peppers

1 tablespoon vinegar

1 tablespoon brandy, such as Brazilian cachaca

1 white onion, thinly sliced

4 tablespoons vegetable oil or lard

3 large cloves garlic, minced

Garnishes

rice:

1/2 cup vegetable oil

1 large clove garlic, minced

6 cups rice

1 tablespoon salt

fruit:

6 oranges

couve a mineira:

5 ounces bacon, coarsely chopped

2 tablespoons vegetable oil

2 cloves garlic, minced

5 pounds kale, stalks removed and finely shredded

farofa:

4 tablespoons butter

4 eggs, beaten

1 teaspoon salt

1 pound manioc flour, or 3 cups bread crumbs

Rinse black beans and soak overnight in cold water to cover. The next morning, place beans, bacon, and bay leaves in a 16- to 20-quart stockpot and cover with water by at least 2 inches. Simmer for 1 hour, checking occasionally to make sure there is enough water to cover the beans. After 1 hour, start adding meats, starting with the beef jerky, followed by the salted pork loin or Canadian bacon, spareribs, sausages, and fresh pork loin. You may need to divide the beans and meats between 2 large pots. Simmer gently for about 1 hour, until beans are tender and fresh pork loin is cooked. Remove 1/2 cup of bean broth from the stockpot and reserve in a small bowl. Remove 2 cups of beans and set aside.

In a mortar, crush red peppers with vinegar and brandy. Add onion and reserved bean broth to make a sauce. Set aside.

In a heavy 10- to-12-inch sauté pan, warm vegetable oil or lard and add garlic, stirring over medium heat for 2 minutes. Add reserved beans to the pan. Mash them with the oil and garlic, stirring in a little of the liquid from the stockpot to make a paste. Mix thoroughly and place the paste in the stockpot to thicken and flavor the beans.

To serve, remove meats from stockpot. Slice each meat into thin slices or individual portions and arrange on a large platter, keeping each meat separate. Serve the beans in a deep earthenware pot, surrounded by the pepper sauce and the following traditional prepared garnishes.

Rice: In a heavy-bottomed saucepan over medium-high heat, heat oil and add garlic. Stir for 2 minutes, then add rice and stir to coat with oil. Add salt and 12 cups of water. Bring to a boil, lower heat, and cook at a gentle simmer, covered, 20 minutes or until rice is tender and liquid has been absorbed.

Fruit: Peel skin and membrane from oranges using a knife. Core them and remove seeds. Slice and chill.

Couve a mineira: In a large sauté pan, cook bacon until crisp; remove from pan and reserve. Discard bacon fat in pan and add vegetable oil and garlic to pan. Add kale and cook over medium-high heat, stirring as the kale cooks down. When the kale is still crisp-tender, remove from heat and stir in bacon pieces. This should be prepared just before serving, so the kale stays crisp and green.

Farofa: Melt butter in a large sauté pan over medium-high heat. Add eggs and salt and stir until they begin to coagulate. Add manioc flour or bread crumbs gradually, stirring constantly. The farofa should remain moist, so add water, 1 teaspoon at a time, if necessary.

Serves 10

For the 11 million residents of Buenos Aires, the Wild West begins just outside of town, on the windswept plains called the Pampas, stretching for hundreds of miles west to the foot of the Andes.

These fertile plains are home to the gauchos, the cowboys who occupy a large part of Argentine legend. Hundreds of years ago, the gauchos were wanderers, rough-hewn and sometimes violent loners who crisscrossed the plains with only a horse and a knife for company. Later, when rich Argentines fenced the plains and put them to work herding cattle, the gauchos' image softened somewhat. Their distinctive garb and skill on horseback still set them apart from the rest of the population. Gauchos traditionally wear wide-brimmed hats with rounded crowns, baggy pants, and calf-high boots. Other details include their wide belts studded with silver coins, flaring leather chaps, woven sashes, and woolen ponchos. In addition to roping and galloping headlong after a stray calf, gauchos are experts at flinging the boleadora, a trio of balls connected with thongs; thrown accurately, the balls can stop a running animal in its tracks.

The huge ranches on the Pampas, known as estancias, were famous for their generous hospitality to travelers, so it is natural that some of the present-day owners have transformed their properties into guest ranches. City people can stay in bedrooms cozily decorated in faded chintz, go horseback riding or dove-shooting, and observe a lifestyle that combines both the civility of the English country house and the unfettered freedom of wide open spaces.

las pampas

argentina

The gauchos' method of cooking meat has become a national tradition of Argentina. This is the asado, an elaborate barbecue with its own techniques of salting various meats and then cooking them slowly on iron frames placed next to, rather than on, a carefully tended wood fire. Afterward, they will share a cup of maté, the tealike drink made of leaves of *Ilex paraguensis*, traditionally made in a gourd and sipped with a metal straw called a bombilla.

chimichurri sauce

salsa

An essential part of every asado is chimichurri sauce, a potent amalgam of oil and vinegar flavored with garlic and chiles. Every parrilla—a restaurant specializing in grilled meat—in the country has a bottle of it on its tables.

1 tablespoon coarse salt

3 tablespoons red pepper flakes

4 cloves garlic, peeled and crushed in a mortar

6 bay leaves

1/2 cup vinegar

3 tablespoons olive oil

Place salt, red pepper flakes, garlic, bay leaves, vinegar, olive oil, and 1/2 cup water in a bottle or flask, and shake to combine. Do not put a stopper in the container. Let stand in a cool place for a day before serving with barbecued meats. It can be sprinkled on the meat while it is cooking or added at the table.

Serves 6

There is nothing minimalist about the colonial city of Puebla, 80 miles east of Mexico City. Almost from the moment that it was founded by the Spaniards in 1513, it has been famous for richly detailed architecture, brilliantly colored ceramics, and elaborate food based on subtle combinations of spices and herbs. The zócalo, bordered on three sides by dignified gray stone arcades, is dominated by the two-towered cathedral incorporating medieval, Renaissance, and neoclassical details.

Two blocks away, the Church of Santo Domingo is a less somber affair, with a sumptuous interior made of curvaceous white stucco carvings shimmering with gold leaf. The church is topped off with a glorious dome covered with Talavera azulejos, hand-painted ceramic tiles that have been made in Puebla since the arrival of Spanish potters in the sixteenth century.

Another confection is the Casa de Alfeñique, a building literally named after a sugarcake; its intricate façade is made of interlaced tiles and brick, all topped off with a white stucco trim that resembles oozing cake frosting.

For Mexican food buffs, the convent of Santa Rosa, now the Museum of Popular Arts, is a pilgrimage site. According to local legend, this cavernous kitchen lined with blue and yellow tiles is where a creative Spanish nun conjured up the rich and spicy sauce known as mole poblano. Like the city's architecture, mole poblano combines both New World materials—chocolate, chiles, and tomatoes—and Old World details, such as cinnamon, cloves, and sesame seeds.

puebla

mexico

Although mole poblano is Puebla's most famous contribution to the cuisine of Mexico, the city also takes credit for Chiles en Nogada, an autumn dish of green chiles stuffed with fruit and meat, bathed in a creamy walnut sauce, and sprinkled with pomegranate seeds to echo the red, white, and green of the national flag. Not all mole sauces are black, and Puebla cooks chop up cilantro, tomatillos, epazote, and purslane to make a vibrant green version.

chicken mole

pollo mole

The list of ingredients may be long, but a blender or food processor shortens the time required for this sauce, which is traditionally served over boiled turkey but may also be served with chicken or pork.

1 3- to 4-pound chicken, cut into 8 pieces

2 teaspoons salt

2 cloves garlic, peeled

1/2 white onion

4 dried mulato chiles

6 dried ancho chiles

4 dried pasilla chiles

3 tablespoons lard or more as needed for frying

1/2 teaspoon anise seeds

1 1/2 tablespoons coriander seeds

1 1/2 tablespoons sesame seeds

2 cloves

1 cinnamon stick, broken into several pieces

2 medium tomatoes

2 cloves garlic, unpeeled

25 raisins

20 whole almonds

1/2 plantain, peeled and cut into thirds

1 thick slice French bread

One bar Ibarra Mexican chocolate

2 tablespoons sesame seeds, toasted

In a 6- to 8-quart stockpot in water to cover, simmer chicken gently over low heat with salt, garlic, and onion. When chicken is done, remove it to a plate and reserve broth.

Remove seeds and veins from chiles and reserve the seeds in a small bowl. In a 10- to 12-inch sauté pan or earthenware pot over medium heat, melt 1 tablespoon of the lard and sauté the chiles briefly. Set them aside in a bowl, pour hot water over them to cover, and soak for 30 minutes to soften. When they have cooled slightly, remove chiles with a slotted spoon to drain and place in a blender or food processor. Blend, adding soaking water as needed to produce a thick liquid.

In a dry pan, toast anise seeds, coriander seeds, sesame seeds, cloves, and cinnamon stick pieces. Allow to cool before grinding the spices very fine in a spice grinder.

Melt 1 tablespoon of lard in the same sauté pan or earthenware pot over medium-high heat, and sauté whole tomatoes and unpeeled garlic until they are browned. Remove tomatoes and garlic; peel garlic. Set aside.

In the same pan, sauté raisins, remove, and set aside. Add almonds to pan, brown lightly, remove, and set aside. Add sliced plantain and bread to pan and brown. Remove and set aside.

In a food processor, blend 2 cups of the reserved chicken broth, browned tomatoes and garlic, raisins, almonds, plantain, and bread.

Melt 1 tablespoon of lard in a 12- to 14-inch sauté pan or earthenware pot over medium heat. Pour in puréed chiles and cook. Add broth mixture to the chiles. Add ground spices. Break chocolate bar into small chunks and add to pan to melt. Cook very slowly, for 3 hours, until mixture cooks down to a thick paste. To serve, dilute the paste with a few tablespoons of the reserved chicken broth. Reheat the chicken pieces and coat with mole sauce. Sprinkle with additional sesame seeds to serve.

Serves 6

In some parts of Mexico these quick and tasty snacks are called chalupas, in other places they're tostadas. Make sure you get the freshest possible corn tortillas, preferably small ones no more than five inches in diameter and hand-patted, if possible. If the idea of frying in lard is not appealing, switch to vegetable or peanut oil.

8 ounces lard or 1 cup vegetable oil

20 small corn tortillas

Salsa Roja and/or Salsa Verde (recipes follow)

8 ounces cooked pork, shredded and heated through

1/2 white onion, chopped

cooked tomato sauce (salsa roja):

4 large ripe tomatoes

2 dried chipotle chiles or 2 fresh serrano chiles

1 clove garlic, peeled

Salt

green sauce (salsa verde):

About 1 teaspoon salt

1 pound fresh tomatillos, husked

4 fresh serrano or jalapeño chiles, or to taste

1/2 cup chopped cilantro

1/4 cup chopped white onion

1 clove garlic, peeled

Warm 3 tablespoons lard or oil over medium-high heat in a large sauté pan. Add as many tortillas as you can fit without overlapping. Cook until lightly browned. Remove and drain on paper towels while you are cooking the rest of the tortillas, adding lard or oil as necessary. Place 2 tortillas on each plate and garnish with pork, a sprinkling of onion and some Salsa Roja or Salsa Verde. Serve immediately.

Cooked Tomato Sauce: In a dry sauté pan over high heat or on a hot griddle, roast tomatoes, turning occasionally, until they are soft. Add chiles, turning until they are lightly browned. Remove blackened skin from tomatoes and from serrano chiles, if using. Place tomatoes, chiles, and garlic in a blender or food processor, and blend until ingredients are uniformly chopped but not puréed. If the sauce is too thick, add a little water. Season to taste with salt.

Green Sauce: In a large saucepan, bring 1 quart water and 1 teaspoon of the salt to a boil. Add tomatillos and chiles, reduce heat, and simmer until they are tender, about 10 minutes. Drain, reserving 1 cup of the liquid. Remove seeds and ribs from chiles. Place tomatillos, chiles, cilantro, onion, and garlic in a blender or food processor, and blend until ingredients are chopped but not puréed. If the sauce is too thick, add a bit of the cooking liquid. Season to taste with salt.

Serves 10

fried tortillas
with two sauces

chalupas poblanas con dos salsas

With a thousand people per square mile, Puerto Rico is crowded, but you would never know it on the southwest coast. Here, between the small cities of Ponce Mayaguez and Rincón lie white sand beaches and tumbling surf, tropical gardens and coffee plantations.

A two-hour drive from the discos and casinos of San Juan, this is the place to admire Puerto Rico's natural attributes. Snorkelers and scuba divers drift for hours above coral reefs, and windsurfers and surfers praise the wind and waves near Rincón as the best in the Caribbean. Campers can visit Mona Island, the protected home of rare sea turtles, iguanas, and ocean birds. The area's lighthouses are places to see humpback whales playing in the tropical waves during their annual winter visits.

Less energetic pleasures near the western shores of Puerto Rico include San Germán, perched in the mountains southeast of Mayaguez. This historic town has not only preserved hundreds of examples of colonial and criollo architecture, but also has retained leisurely customs like the paseo, the ritual evening stroll around the plazas. The Iglesia Porta Coeli, one of the oldest churches in the Western Hemisphere, houses religious art from around the world, notably a collection of santos, the carved wooden figures that are an ancient folk art tradition. Another Puerto Rican tradition, the lace called mundillo, requiring the manipulation of dozens of bobbins, originally came to the island from Spain and Belgium and still survives in Mayaguez and other towns in the western section of the island.

southwest

puerto rico

In the mid-nineteenth century, coffee grown in the western mountains of Puerto Rico was considered the finest in the world by popes, kings, and connoisseurs. Fifty years later, the industry was all but devastated by hurricanes, war, and tariffs, and Puerto Rican coffee was strictly for home consumption. Recently, however, some growers have begun producing high-grade beans again; experts have ranked their beans with the likes of Jamaica Blue Mountain and Kona, and Puerto Rico is exporting coffee to the world again.

seafood soup

asopao de mariscos

Puerto Ricans love their asopaos, not quite soups, not quite

stews, but something in between—in this case, red snapper

and shellfish in a thick liquid filled with vegetables.

6 cups fish stock

3 tablespoons roux, made with olive oil and flour

1/4 cup julienned carrots

1/4 cup julienned zucchini

1/4 cup julienned yellow squash

1/4 cup thinly sliced Spanish red onion

1 teaspoon cajun spice

1 teaspoon dried basil

4 tablespoons clarified butter

1 pound red snapper fillets, cut in large cubes

16 mussels, removed from shells

16 scallops

8 medium shrimp, peeled and deveined

Salt and pepper

Heat fish stock in a 6- to 8-quart pot, and whisk in roux to thicken. Add carrots, zucchini, squash, onion, cajun spice, and basil, and simmer on low heat while you prepare the fish.

Melt 2 tablespoons of clarified butter in a 12- to 14-inch sauté pan over medium heat, and add fish. Cook, shaking occasionally, until fish is almost cooked through, about 5 minutes (it should be opaque but still moist looking in the center). Add fish to stock mixture.

Melt 2 more tablespoons of clarified butter in the pan, and add mussels, scallops, and shrimp. Shake the pan until they are cooked, 3 to 4 minutes, then add the seafood to the fish stock. Taste for seasoning, and add salt and pepper to taste. Serve immediately.

Serves 4

The tropical intensity and sweetness of mango and the crisp sharpness of onions and peppers are combined in a sauce that enhances fresh fish that is partly grilled, then finished in the oven. A simple stir-fry of readily available vegetables adds color to the presentation.

mango sauce:

1 cup diced ripe mango

2 tablespoons minced cilantro

2 tablespoons diced green bell pepper

2 tablespoons diced red bell pepper

2 tablespoons diced Spanish red onion

2 tablespoons finely chopped scallions

1/4 cup olive oil

Salt and pepper

snapper:

1/4 cup olive oil

1 tablespoon minced garlic

6 8-ounce red snapper fillets

1 teaspoon dried basil

Salt and pepper

side dish:

2 tablespoons olive oil

1/2 cup julienned carrots

1/2 cup julienned zucchini

1/2 cup julienned yellow squash

1/2 cup thinly sliced Spanish red onion

4 potatoes, cooked and cut in half

To make mango sauce, in a bowl, combine mango with cilantro, peppers, onion, and scallions. Stir in olive oil and salt and pepper to taste. Refrigerate overnight before serving.

To prepare the snapper, mix olive oil and garlic, and brush this mixture on one side of fish fillets. Sprinkle with dried basil and salt and pepper to taste. Place each fillet on a very hot grill, seasoned side down. Season the other side. After 3 minutes, rotate each fillet a quarter turn. Grill for about 6 minutes, until fish is three-quarters cooked, and remove fish to a baking dish. Finish cooking in a preheated 400°F oven for about 5 minutes.

Meanwhile, to make the side dish, warm olive oil in a large sauté pan over medium heat. Add vegetables and potatoes, and cook, stirring or shaking occasionally, for about 5 minutes.

Serve fish immediately, with vegetables and potatoes and mango sauce on the side.

Serves 6

grilled snapper
with mango sauce

huachinango con salsa de mango

index

C

tributes

After the success of *Avventura: Journeys in Italian Cuisine*, it was hard to resist creating another fun-filled series packed with sights and gastronomic delights. *Entrada: Journeys in Latin American Cuisine* was the resulting adventure for our Gourmet Excursions team. Our mission is to help you experience the world through an ongoing journey in your very own kitchen. We are certain that *Entrada* will bring you closer to the many flavorful cultures of Latin America.

I would like to give special thanks to the following people for their vision and continued energy: Supervising Producer, Toni Stevens; Producer, Dorothy Engelman; Director, Craig Moffit; and Host, Roanna Sabeh-Azar.

The production of *Entrada*, like any television series, required the efforts of a special group of skilled individuals. We are grateful to the *Entrada* production team and the equally committed teams at Catalyst and Gullane Entertainment for their talent and support. Thank you to all of the guests and people who helped to make *Entrada* such a success.

We would also like to thank Bay Books and all of the television stations worldwide for broadcasting *Entrada: Journeys in Latin American Cuisine*.

In closing, this book is dedicated to the many charismatic chefs and unique restaurants that provided our inspiration for the serie:

Thank you,
Charles Falzon, Executive Producer

None of this would have been possible without all of these amazing chefs: ¡Muchas Gracias!

Israel Perez Cruz
Nelida Diaz
Hugo "Perla" Salas
Vanessa Musi Batty
Connie Alda
Maria Elena Lyon Valverde
Yara Castro Roberts
Teresa Peralta
Joaquina Silva Vacas
Felipe Goroito
Rhonda Tranks
Ruth Von Waerebeek
Maggie Alarcon
Juan Demuru
Murillo Brocchini
Mariano Ortiz
Pablo Massey
Iliana de la Vega Arnaud
Carmen Granado
Ana Castilho
Luis Torres Hernandez
Martiriano Ekayin
Marcella Ortiz
Ana Elena Martinez
Johnny Quinones
José Alfredo Martinez Esquivel